DINOSAUR EXPLORERS

INFOGRAPHICS
FOR DISCOVERING
THE PREHISTORIC WORLD

Text by

CRISTINA BANFI

Illustrations by

GIULIA DE AMICIS

SHELTER HARBOR PRESS
NEW YORK

INTRODUCTION

Are you crazy about dinosaurs? Would you say you're a fellow sufferer of dinomania? If the answer's yes, then this book's definitely for you, because it's jam-packed with pictures and information about the many different dinosaurs that lived here on Earth. Dinosaurs first appeared on our planet millions of years ago, and they went extinct during the Cretaceous period, the last period of the Mesozoic era. In general, most dinosaurs were very large and heavy, but some were no bigger than chickens!

The pages in this book will explain what dinosaurs were like and how they went extinct. Which time periods did dinosaurs live in? What did they eat? And if they're all gone now, how do we even know they existed? Rich, up-to-date charts and diagrams bring all this information and more to life in a fun and interesting way.

Whenever possible, dinosaurs and other prehistoric animals are compared to present-day animals to make the information more accessible. By the end of the book, you'll understand more about the science and history behind dinosaurs and why scientists and paleontologists have been studying them to this day.

THE EVOLUTION OF DINOSAURS

Everybody knows dinosaurs. We usually imagine them as gigantic, scary lizards tearing apart their prey during the few years they lived here on Earth. In reality, dinosaurs came in all shapes and sizes, and they lived during a long geological era that paleontologists call the Mesozoic era.

NOT ONLY DINOSAURS

Now completely extinct, dinosaurs lived in a period between 245 and 65 million years ago (mya), **but not all Mesozoic animals were dinosaurs**. Dinosaurs shared their habitats with many other animals, including birds, mammals, and insects.

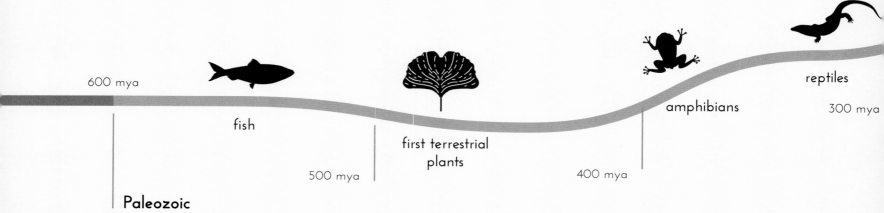

600 mya

fish

first terrestrial plants

500 mya

amphibians

reptiles

300 mya

400 mya

Paleozoic

WHAT MAKES A DINOSAUR?

1 Dinosaurs **lived only during the Mesozoic era**. Any animal present on Earth outside of this era can't officially be called a dinosaur.

2 All dinosaurs lived on land.
Even though some dinosaurs could swim short distances, they never lived permanently in lakes, seas, or rivers like fish or crustaceans. Many big marine reptiles lived during the Mesozoic era, but we don't call them dinosaurs. Even those huge, fast-flying reptiles known as pterosaurs weren't actually dinosaurs—they were really just flying reptiles!

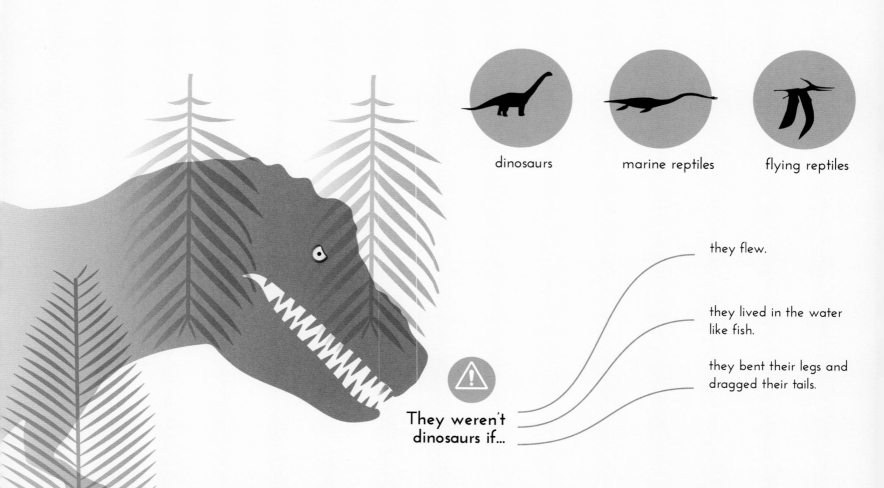

dinosaurs

marine reptiles

flying reptiles

they flew.

they lived in the water like fish.

they bent their legs and dragged their tails.

They weren't dinosaurs if...

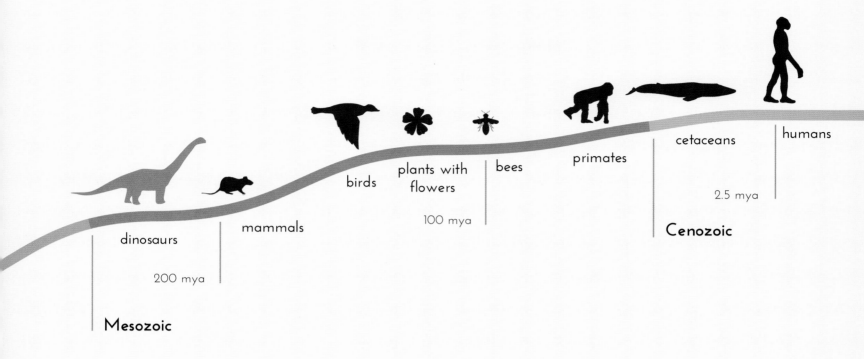

birds

plants with flowers

100 mya

bees

primates

cetaceans

2.5 mya

humans

dinosaurs

200 mya

Mesozoic

mammals

Cenozoic

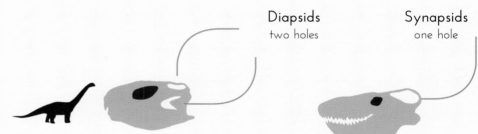

Diapsids
two holes

Synapsids
one hole

Anapsids
no hole

3 Dinosaurs walked on land. Their legs were positioned directly underneath their body, keeping it raised from the ground. Many mammals and birds alive today have the same characteristic. This adaptation made **dinosaurs excellent walkers and runners** and probably helped them survive for so many millions of years.

4 **All dinosaurs were diapsids**, meaning their skulls had two holes (or fenestrae) behind their eye sockets. These holes made their heads lighter and allowed room for the development of their jaw muscles. Many reptiles were synapsids, meaning their skulls had only one hole. Others were anapsids (no holes).

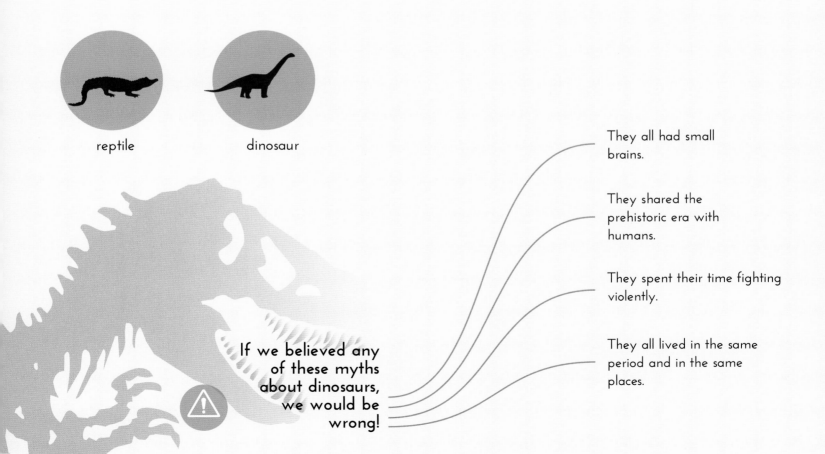

reptile

dinosaur

If we believed any of these myths about dinosaurs, we would be wrong!

They all had small brains.

They shared the prehistoric era with humans.

They spent their time fighting violently.

They all lived in the same period and in the same places.

THE CLASSIFICATION

What kind of dinosaur are you?

Dinosaurs were very different from one another in shape and size. Therefore, it's difficult to classify them rigidly, especially considering we only have their fossils to study. It's up to scientists to identify certain characteristics in plants and animals and then to sort them into groups. In 1888, the English paleontologist Harry Seeley invented a dinosaur classification system that is still used today. Based on the size and shape of the dinosaur's pelvic bones, it's sorted into one of two groups, which are called "orders." One group is called Ornithischia, or "bird-hipped," and the other is called Saurischia, or "reptile-hipped."

DINOSAUR
ORDERS

The pelvis is made up of three bones joined together: the ilium, the ischium, and the pubis.

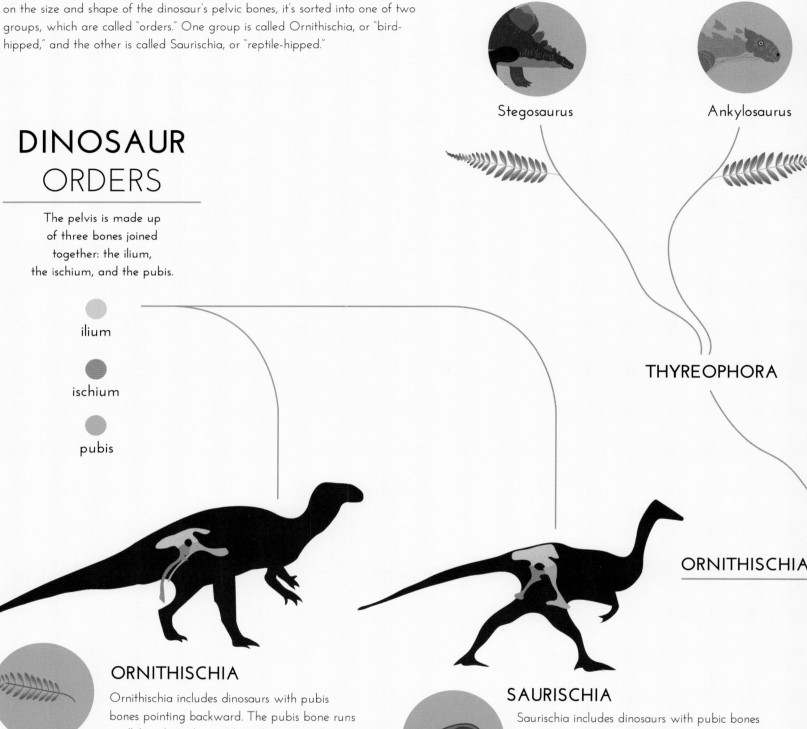

Stegosaurus

Ankylosaurus

ilium

ischium

pubis

THYREOPHORA

ORNITHISCHIA

ORNITHISCHIA

Ornithischia includes dinosaurs with pubis bones pointing backward. The pubis bone runs parallel to the ischium. The ischium is in the upper part of the hip and tends to be long and narrow. Noncarnivorous dinosaurs belong to this order. The shape of their pelvises allowed plenty of space for their large intestines, which were massive and complex because of all the plants they were digesting.

SAURISCHIA

Saurischia includes dinosaurs with pubic bones that pointed forward between the legs, which gave them more support for greater speed and strength. These dinosaurs were mostly meat-eaters and therefore had to move quickly if they wanted to hunt. The ilium in the upper part of the hip was large and flat, and that's what their powerful leg muscles were connected to.

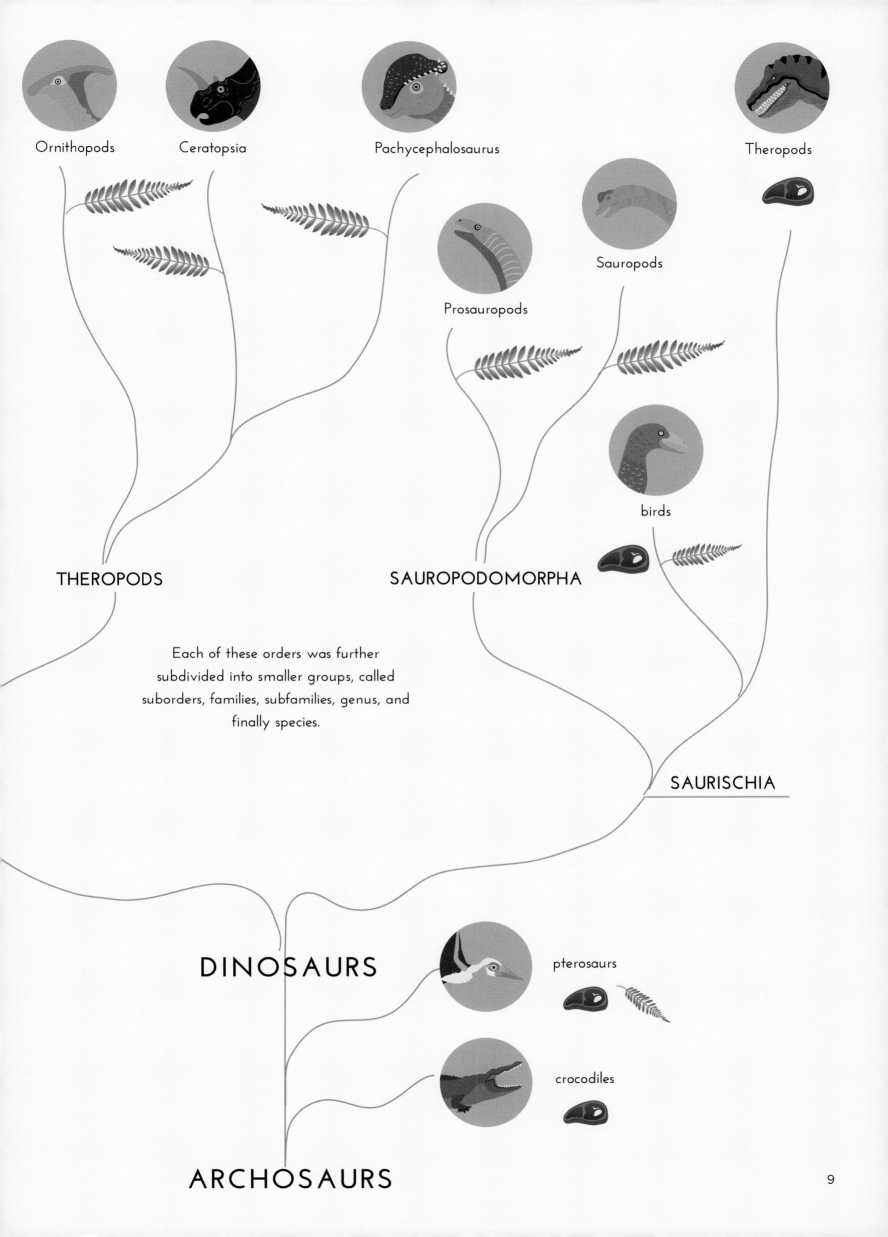

Ornithopods

Ceratopsia

Pachycephalosaurus

Theropods

Prosauropods

Sauropods

birds

THEROPODS

SAUROPODOMORPHA

Each of these orders was further subdivided into smaller groups, called suborders, families, subfamilies, genus, and finally species.

SAURISCHIA

DINOSAURS

pterosaurs

crocodiles

ARCHOSAURS

THE ERA OF DINOSAURS

As you surely know already, there are no dinosaurs on Earth today.

They haven't existed on our planet for 65 million years, but there was a time when these creatures thrived, living in many different habitats around the world and surviving in many different ways. Paleontologists call the period of the dinosaurs, which lasted for 186 million years, the Mesozoic era, or simply the Mesozoic.

The Mesozoic era (186 million years) has been divided by paleontologists into three shorter periods: the Triassic period, the Jurassic period, and the Cretaceous period.

TRIASSIC

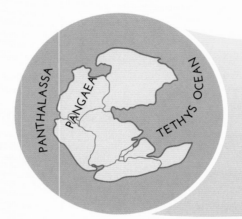

The Triassic period lasted for 51 million years and began with a massive extinction event—possibly the largest one that has ever occurred. The Earth became almost completely uninhabited: 96 percent of marine species went extinct, as well as 70 percent of terrestrial vertebrates.

TRIASSIC

Early Triassic

The Earth's landmass is concentrated into one massive continent, Pangaea, which is surrounded by an immense ocean, the Panthalassa.

Late Triassic

The Earth begins to heat up, thus becoming an ideal habitat for reptiles. Archosaurs become the dominant land vertebrates, a subclass that also includes the dinosaurs and the pterosaurs.

MESOZOIC
duration: 186 million years

| 251 mya | Triassic | 204 mya | Jurassic | 146 mya | Cretaceous | 65 mya |

mya = million years ago

Think about this for a minute: the dinosaurs
that lived in the Triassic period, such as the
herbivorous Plateosaurus, are further away in
time from the carnivore T. rex (Tyrannosaurus
rex) than T. rex is from us!

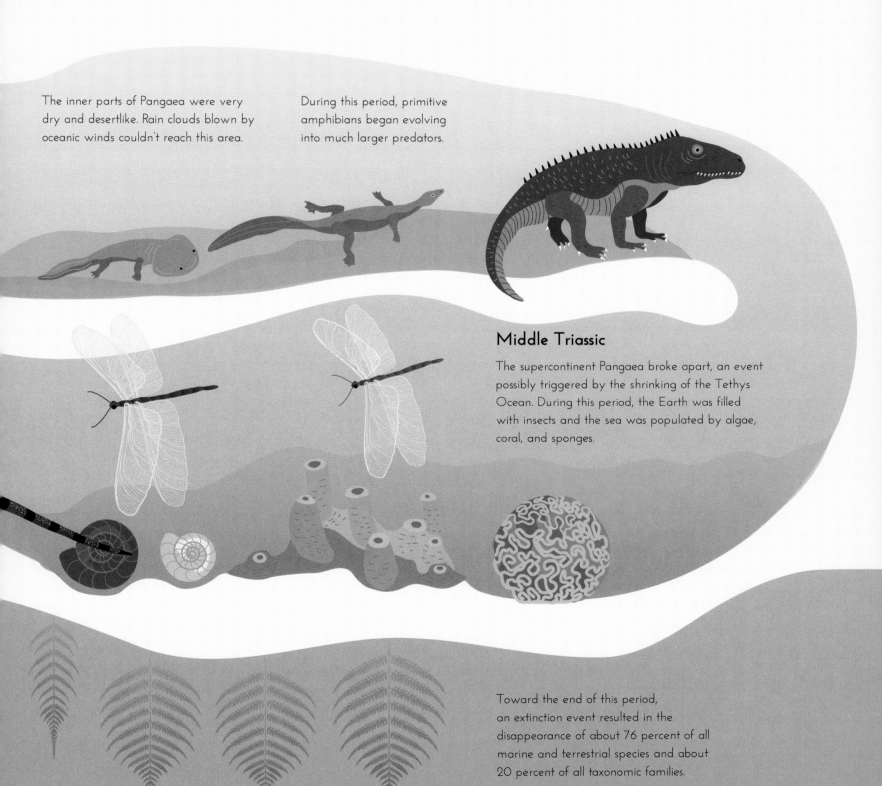

The inner parts of Pangaea were very
dry and desertlike. Rain clouds blown by
oceanic winds couldn't reach this area.

During this period, primitive
amphibians began evolving
into much larger predators.

Middle Triassic

The supercontinent Pangaea broke apart, an event
possibly triggered by the shrinking of the Tethys
Ocean. During this period, the Earth was filled
with insects and the sea was populated by algae,
coral, and sponges.

Toward the end of this period,
an extinction event resulted in the
disappearance of about 76 percent of all
marine and terrestrial species and about
20 percent of all taxonomic families.

JURASSIC

The Jurassic period, which lasted for 55 million years, began with an extinction. The Earth started to get warmer and warmer.

Early Jurassic

The climate was warm and mild. Archosaurus (and other reptiles) dominated the Earth. The first mammals began to appear at this time, though they were generally very small and only occupied areas that weren't dominated by reptiles.

Middle Jurassic

Pangaea no longer exists. It's now divided into two continents: Laurasia and Gondwana.

Early Cretaceous

The ocean levels rose significantly, taking over many lands on the two continents and reducing the size of many forested areas. This development has a negative effect on the massive sauropods, which eventually go extinct.

During this period, Earth began to take on its regular seasons. The poles got colder with every passing winter. Plants with flowers appeared, along with common insects like bees and ants. Mammals continued to evolve, eventually developing the placenta, which leads to the development of many new mammalian species.

CRETACEOUS

Lasting 80 million years, this is the longest period of the Mesozoic era. Many dinosaurs are now extinct, while lots of other animals and insects continue to evolve and diversify. The first birds with beaks and no teeth appear.

Dinosaurs have reached their peak. This changes with a massive extinction event called the "K-T extinction," which finishes off many of Earth's last great dinosaurs.

The gigantic sauropods and many other dinosaurs, including both carnivores and herbivores (though grass doesn't exist yet!), walked the surface of the Earth.

The big forests on Earth were mostly made up of conifer trees. Marine reptiles and ammonites thrived in the seas. Pterosaurs ruled the skies.

Late Jurassic

Dinosaurs kept diversifying in shape and size. The first birds appeared, including Archaeopteryx. The sea levels continued to rise, serving as a home for many new life-forms.

Late Cretaceous

This is the final act of the Mesozoic era. Earth's temperature begins to drop, and this continues into the next era. Many dinosaurs, including Ankylosaurus, Triceratops, and Tyrannosaurus rex, are at the peak of their evolutionary success.

Their story ends with the great K-T extinction, which wipes out more than just dinosaurs! Almost three-quarters of all plant and animal species living on Earth went extinct. Reptilian rule is over, and it's now time for mammals to take control. Very slowly, they begin to conquer the planet.

THE GREAT EXTINCTION

The last dinosaurs disappeared 65 million years ago in circumstances that still haven't been fully explained. Many theories exist about what exactly finished them off. Was it a meteor? Environmental changes? Gases pouring out of volcanoes? Whatever the initial culprit, it was probably a combination of different things that caused them to die off.

How did it happen? We can only make hypotheses...

THE IMPACT OF A METEORITE

There is evidence that a huge meteorite struck the Earth near the Gulf of Mexico 65 million years ago. The impact may have raised 70 billion tons of dust and debris, which could have blocked out the sunlight for an extended period. This would have caused temperatures to drop by as much as 47°F. On a now-icy planet without the sunlight to help photosynthesis, many plants would have died, which in turn would have killed off many herbivores. And without the herbivores to feed on, the carnivores would have eventually died out, too.

CLIMATE CHANGE

The impact of the meteorite also further broke up the continents. It changed Earth's climate dramatically, making it less hospitable to reptilian creatures like dinosaurs.

CATASTROPHIC GEOLOGICAL EVENTS

At the end of the Mesozoic era, the Earth underwent a period of geological instability that included changing temperatures, strong earthquakes, and violent volcanic eruptions that filled the air with ash and gas and made it harder for land animals to breathe.

NEW PLANTS AND ANIMALS

The appearance of plants with flowers created many problems in the food chain. Because flowering plants lost their leaves during the fall, many dinosaurs starved to death during those long months.

DINOSAURS
UNDER THE X-RAY

The dinosaur remains discovered thus far have almost always been the hardest parts of their bodies, such as the bones or the teeth, which have managed to resist decomposition.

The process of organic material (organs, skin) becoming inorganic material (calcium, minerals) is called "mineralization." The most common dinosaur fossils are the mineralized remains of bones, claws, and horns.

In order to study the missing organs of dinosaurs, scientists make comparisons with existing animals, in particular with those that closely resemble dinosaurs, including many bird and reptile species.

 1 bones

 2 claws

3 horns

DINOSAUR ORGANS

THE HEART

Blood circulation happened in dinosaurs thanks to the constant pumping of their heart, the size of which varied depending on the size of the dinosaur.

T. rex

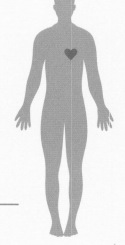

T. rex likely had a heart 10 times larger than that of a human!

Mammal and bird hearts are made up of two completely separate atrium-ventricle pairs that create a powerful double-pump. This kind of heart supports a very active lifestyle. What about dinosaur hearts? According to paleontologists, their hearts were actually very similar to modern-day bird hearts.

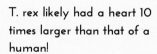

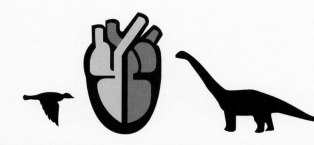

The sauropods had truly enormous hearts that likely weighed as much as 63 pounds.

THE LUNGS

The respiratory function in carnivorous dinosaurs had to be very efficient in order to provide all the oxygen necessary while chasing down prey or running from another predator. When the great predators like T. rex took a breath, the air likely went through the lungs and directly into a complex web of air sacs similar to the ones birds have. Such a system would have guaranteed a larger intake of oxygen with every breath.

air sacs

THE BRAIN

How an animal lives and moves within its environment mainly depends on the shape and size of its brain, and this fact applies to dinosaurs, too. Dinosaurs generally had brains that were much smaller than those of mammals or birds of the same size. For a long time, many people believed that this meant they were unintelligent creatures.

However, the traces they left behind indicate that they were animals with complex behaviors. They likely cared for their young and had social interactions with other dinosaurs. The brains of predators were most likely larger, as they would have needed the extra smarts to develop hunting strategies. Modern-day reptiles have brains that are probably similar to the ones dinosaurs had.

Troodon is an exception. It had a very large brain considering its small size, which suggests that it was probably more intelligent than your average dinosaur and maybe even as clever as a few modern-day birds, such as the blackbird or the magpie.

STOMACH AND INTESTINES

The digestive system of dinosaurs varied depending on whether they were a carnivore or a herbivore.

HERBIVORE DIET

In order to store lots of plant matter, dinosaur stomachs had to be big, almost like huge bags. Like modern herbivorous birds and crocodiles, some dinosaurs would swallow small stones (called "gastroliths") to help grind up and digest the food in their gastrointestinal tract. The powerful muscles on the walls of the stomach would mix the leaves with the stones and break down the food into smaller pieces.

It's believed that herbivorous dinosaurs had long intestines to help digest all the plants they ate, which were made of cellulose—a very resistant nutrient that was hard to digest.

stomach

intestine

gastrolith

CARNIVORE DIET

Carnivores probably had much simpler digestive systems. This is because the digestion of meat is quite fast compared to that of plants. The intestines of carnivores were likely tucked under the pelvis so as not to get in the way when the dinosaur was moving or running.

18

THE SENSES: SIGHT, SMELL, AND HEARING

Paleontologists study dinosaur senses by looking at their skulls. More specifically, they analyze the imprints their brains left behind on the walls of their skulls, which gives us clues about what each dinosaur brain was capable of.

SIGHT

Herbivores generally had eyes on both sides of their head. This is typical of animals that have many predators. Having an eye on each side allows for a wider range of vision, which helps the animal spot predators.

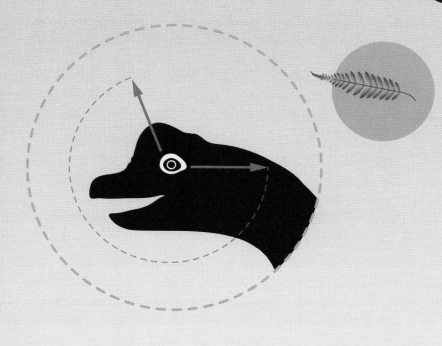

Carnivores often had large eyes that faced straight ahead. Normally their eyes had stereoscopic (or three-dimensional) vision. This helped them gauge the distance of prey with greater accuracy and determine how fast they would need to run in order to catch them.

SMELL

 The olfactory lobe (the part of the brain responsible for smell) of most dinosaurs was generally large, leading us to believe that smell was critical for dinosaurs to find food or recognize members of their own species.

HEARING

 We know very little about dinosaur hearing. Like modern reptiles and birds, dinosaurs didn't have outer ears. Their middle or inner ears were likely highly developed.

Baby dinosaurs could probably detect high-frequency sounds, almost like dogs or dolphins, while adult dinosaurs were likely sensitive to infrasound (or low-frequency sounds), which they may have used for long-distance communication, much like elephants or whales.

DINOSAUR WEIGHTS AND SIZES

The word "dinosaur" brings to mind terrifying reptiles with gigantic, heavy bodies that caused the ground to tremble with every step. The Earth was of course populated by many large dinosaurs, but there were also plenty of dinosaurs with sizes similar to those of common modern-day animals.

Which was the biggest?
Which was the smallest?
Which was the heaviest?
Well, it's complicated...

LENGTH

How do we calculate the size of a dinosaur? Measuring the length seems like the easiest way, right? All we would have to do is measure the skeleton. However, because dinosaurs went extinct millions of years ago, scientists very rarely have complete skeletons available to study, so the dimensions have to be estimated based on the (often very few) bones that have been discovered.

78 feet
Brontosaurus

HERBIVORES

We do know for sure that certain species reached truly gigantic proportions, like the sauropods, which probably would have been able to peek through the third-floor window of a tall building.

85 feet
Diplodocus

26 feet
Triceratops

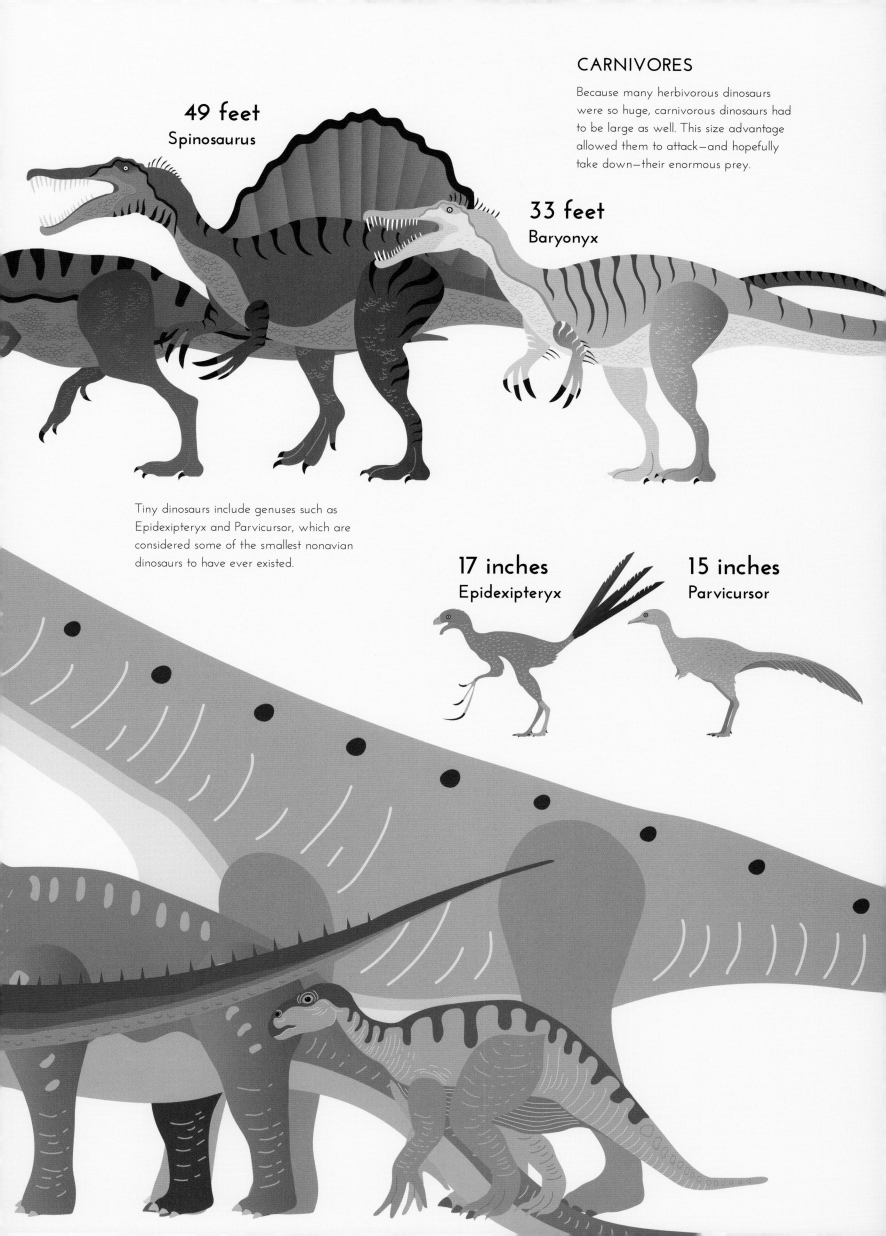

49 feet
Spinosaurus

33 feet
Baryonyx

CARNIVORES

Because many herbivorous dinosaurs were so huge, carnivorous dinosaurs had to be large as well. This size advantage allowed them to attack—and hopefully take down—their enormous prey.

Tiny dinosaurs include genuses such as Epidexipteryx and Parvicursor, which are considered some of the smallest nonavian dinosaurs to have ever existed.

17 inches
Epidexipteryx

15 inches
Parvicursor

WEIGHT

Paleontologists have to use math to find dinosaur weights. By measuring the length of certain bones, such as the femur, they can estimate how much weight such an important structural bone would have been able to support. Paleontologists estimate that sauropods weighed somewhere around 77 tons, which is about half the weight of a blue whale, the largest animal alive today.

6.6 tons
African elephant

44 tons
Boeing 737

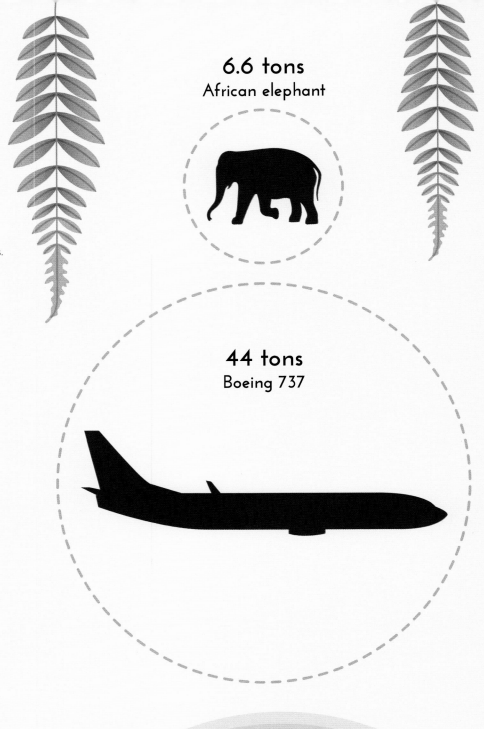

11 tons
Tyrannosaurus

16.5 tons
Diplodocus

38 tons
Brachiosaurus

55 ton
Argentinosaurus

77 tons
Lingwulong shenqi

DINOSAUR SMILES:
TEETH AND FANGS

Animal teeth give us clues about the foods the particular animal liked to eat and where it found them.

Some teeth are perfect for tearing apart plants, while others are meant for biting into prey. The size, shape, and number of teeth reveal a lot about the animal.

Dinosaur species have even been discovered with no teeth, and these are particularly challenging for paleontologists to study, as their diets often remain a mystery. Some dinosaurs had beaks instead of teeth, but usually these sharp beaks were used to pick apart leaves and plants instead of other animals.

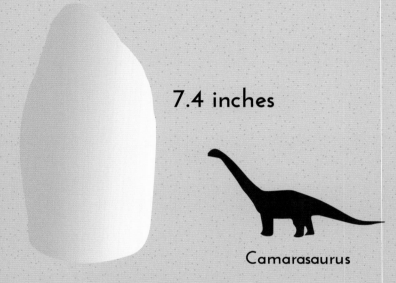

7.4 inches
Camarasaurus

7.4 inches
Diplodocus

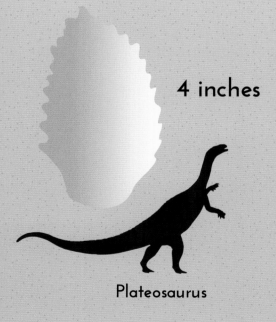

4 inches
Plateosaurus

5 inches
Spinosaurus

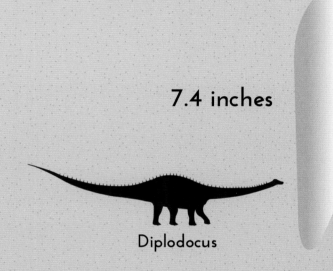

3 inches
Allosaurus

Many dinosaurs were capable of regrowing their teeth. The broken or worn-out ones would periodically fall out, only to be replaced by razor-sharp new ones.

Because there were so many types of dinosaurs, dinosaur teeth vary greatly in size and shape—there's really no standard size!

In some dinosaur species, a small number of teeth were set far apart from each other, while in others the teeth formed close rows, almost like the seats in a movie theater. Some species had more teeth in the front of their mouths, and others had more in the back.

CARNIVORES

Predators like the theropods had pointed teeth: some were straight, while others were curved. Very often their teeth had serrated edges capable of tearing holes into the flesh of their prey. The teeth of carnivores were not really meant for chewing. They were meant for taking their victims down or holding them in place, and many carnivores would even swallow their victims whole or in large chunks, much like sharks or crocodiles.

T. rex teeth could each reach the size of a banana! Normally they had 50-60 teeth, and each played a different role depending on its position in the mouth. T. rex's front teeth would grab hold of the prey. Its center teeth would tear through or chew flesh. And its back teeth helped push the food down its throat.

Cone-shaped, nonserrated teeth indicate that the dinosaur fed on fish instead of other land animals. Spinosaurus, which had teeth similar to those of a crocodile, is a good example of this.

12 inches
T. rex tooth
(scale 1:1)

The largest dinosaur tooth on record belongs to T. rex. It measures 12 inches!

Enamel

Root

0.4 inch
Human

3 inches

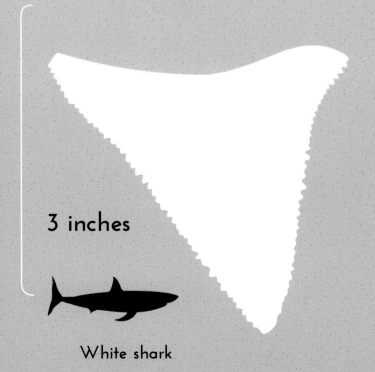

White shark

HERBIVORES

Many herbivorous dinosaurs had horned beaks or very small teeth.

However, the teeth of Triceratops were huge. Positioned in long lines, they acted almost like scissors, helping Triceratops cut through leaves and plant matter.

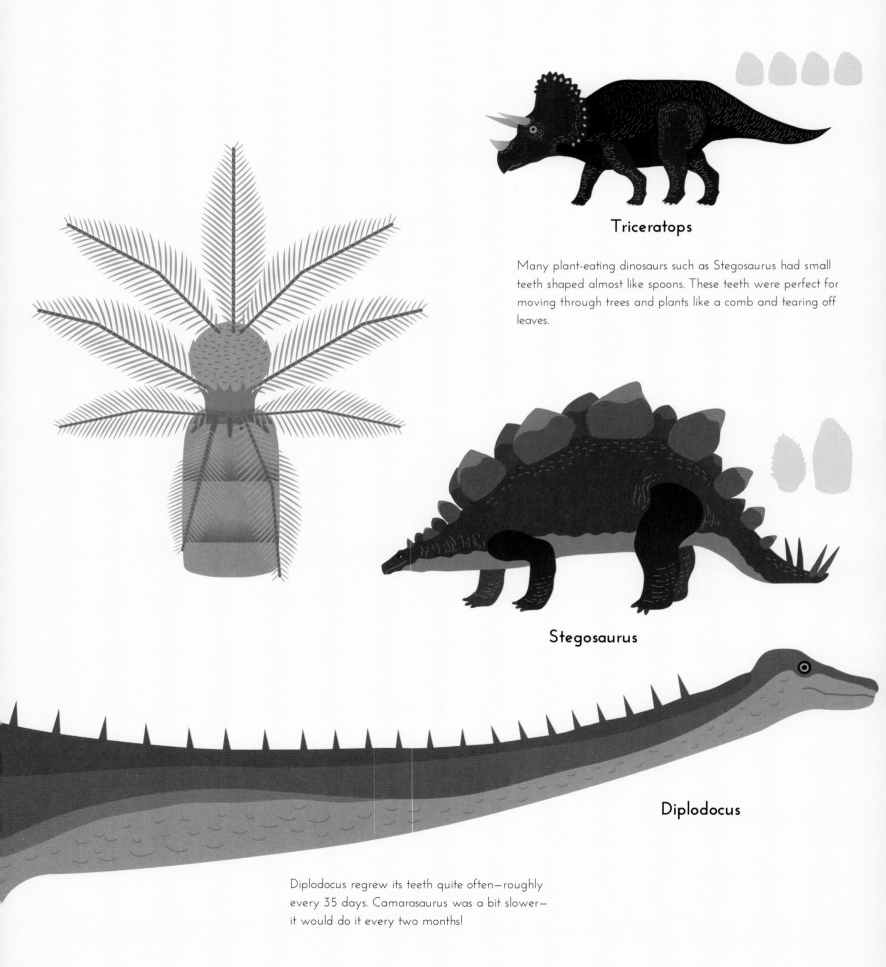

Triceratops

Many plant-eating dinosaurs such as Stegosaurus had small teeth shaped almost like spoons. These teeth were perfect for moving through trees and plants like a comb and tearing off leaves.

Stegosaurus

Diplodocus

Diplodocus regrew its teeth quite often—roughly every 35 days. Camarasaurus was a bit slower— it would do it every two months!

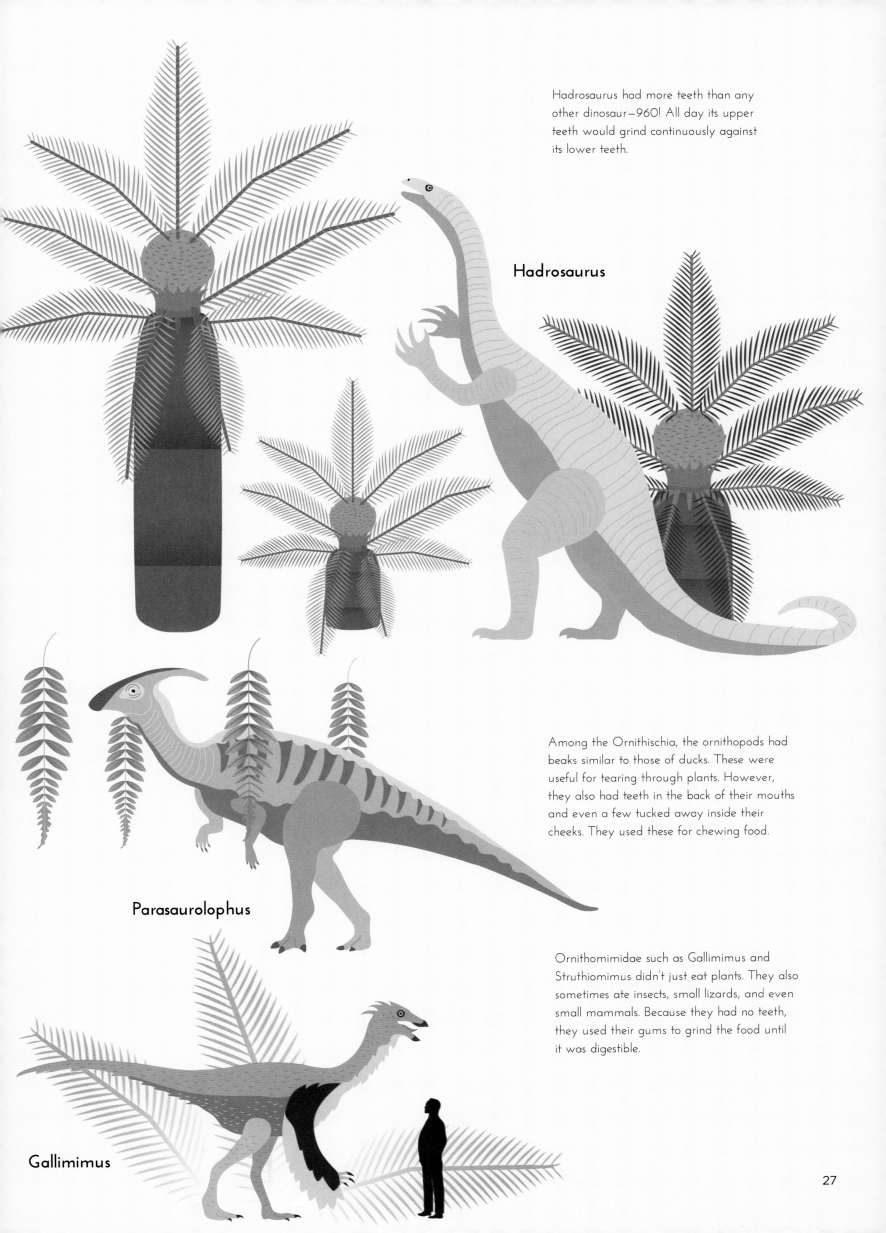

Hadrosaurus had more teeth than any other dinosaur—960! All day its upper teeth would grind continuously against its lower teeth.

Hadrosaurus

Among the Ornithischia, the ornithopods had beaks similar to those of ducks. These were useful for tearing through plants. However, they also had teeth in the back of their mouths and even a few tucked away inside their cheeks. They used these for chewing food.

Parasaurolophus

Ornithomimidae such as Gallimimus and Struthiomimus didn't just eat plants. They also sometimes ate insects, small lizards, and even small mammals. Because they had no teeth, they used their gums to grind the food until it was digestible.

Gallimimus

SPIKES, ARMOR,
AND OTHER DEFENSES

In the food chain, herbivores are always prey, and this rule also applies to dinosaurs. Being prey led to the need to develop protections and defenses in order to survive against carnivores. The more sophisticated these defenses were, the higher the chances of survival.

Some species became faster. Others learned to stay in large groups, adopting a "strength in numbers" approach similar to that of the wildebeest living in Africa. Many also developed bodily defenses that allowed them to fight off attackers. These defenses included horns, claws, clubs, and spikes.

WHIPS!

Sauropods weren't attacked very often due to their enormous size. However, if they were attacked, they could snap their long tails like whips, keeping predators at a distance.

Supersaurus and Brachiosaurus defended themselves with their strong, whiplike tails.

ARMOR UP

Dinosaur armor came in many different shapes and sizes and was generally made of strong plates of bone known as "osteoderms" or "scutes." Today, animals such as crocodiles and armadillos have developed similar protections.

Some dinosaurs grew spikes on their bodies for protection. Normally these grew along their backs and sides, but some also had them on their tails, heads, and faces! Dinosaurs with spikes, such as Stegosaurus, were often very slow-moving. Because of this, they rarely attacked other dinosaurs. Most of the time, their spikes were used only to discourage predators from trying to bite them.

Dinosaurs with heavy plates on their backs are naturally called "armored dinosaurs." Ankylosaurus is probably the most famous armored dinosaur. The weight of their heavy armor meant that they couldn't move much faster than 6 miles per hour. These untouchable dinosaurs were like small tanks!

Ankylosaurus

Scelidosaurus

Stegosaurus

Ankylosaurus

Cretaceous

Further development of spikes and plates on the back, shoulders, and tail of many species.

Early Jurassic

Rows of bony scutes begin to appear on the backs of many dinosaur species.

Late Jurassic

Certain species develop spikes or plates on their backs and shoulders, along with spiked tails.

The club tail of Ankylosaurus.

CLUB TAILS

No modern reptile has a defensive tail quite like that of the Ankylosaurus. The big club was positioned at the tip of its tail. It was made of several bones fused together into one large piece.

Thanks to Ankylosaurus' powerful tail muscles, its club had no trouble swinging from one side to the other. If a predator was hit by this swinging club, the damage could be severe, and sometimes even fatal.

The triangular plates of Stegosaurus.

The spikes of Kentrosaurus could each measure 23 inches long!

SPIKES AND PLATES

Many dinosaurs like Kentrosaurus developed double rows of triangular plates along their backs. The plates would start at their necks and run all the way down to the ends of their tails.

Kentrosaurus

The tips of their tails often featured two to four spikes, with some measuring 3 feet long. These sharp spikes could be painful to predators!

Bajadasaurus

Bajadasaurus was another spiked dinosaur. A 32-foot-long sauropod found in Argentina, it grew spikes along its neck, which were extensions of its neck vertebrae. The spikes discouraged predators from biting its long neck.

HORNS

The most famous horned dinosaur is Triceratops, which is from the Ceratopsidae family. Its three large horns were made of solid bone and grew directly out of its skull. The horns above its eye sockets could reach up to 4 feet long, with base diameters of 12 inches each.

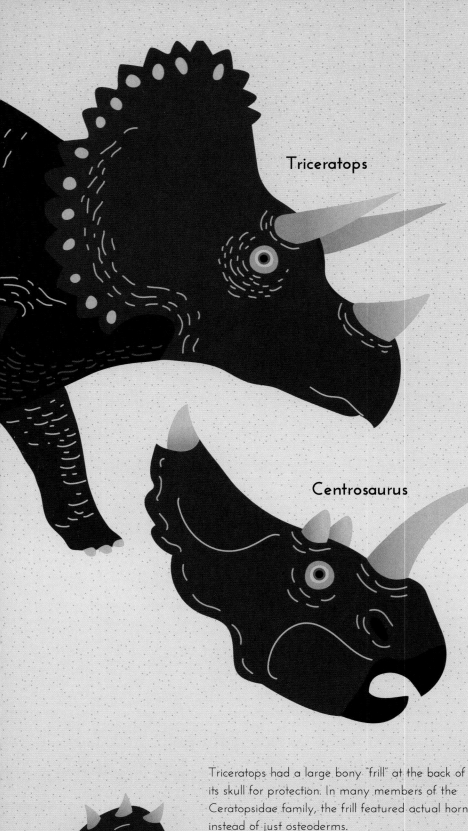

Triceratops

Centrosaurus

Triceratops had a large bony "frill" at the back of its skull for protection. In many members of the Ceratopsidae family, the frill featured actual horns instead of just osteoderms.

Pentaceratops

4 feet

Thanks to these huge horns, Triceratops' head could weigh up to half a ton. But despite this incredible weight, the strong joints in its skull allowed it to move its head in all directions, making the horns a powerful weapon against predators. Some paleontologists believe the force of Triceratops' horns would have been strong enough to break through the side of a car!

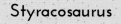

Styracosaurus

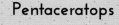

Triceratops was a defensive dinosaur, sometimes even against members of its own group. When under attack, the biggest and strongest individuals within the group would generally surround the younger and more vulnerable members, pointing their horns at predators. Modern-day musk oxen display similar behaviors as they defend themselves against wolves.

CLAWS

Some species of dinosaurs had claws on their rear limbs, which they used for grabbing hold of plants.

Iguanodon is one example. About 33 feet long, these large herbivores fed on huge quantities of leaves. To lower tree branches, they probably used the conical thumbs on their hands, which were much larger and sharper than their other fingers.

It's likely Iguanodon used these strange claws as weapons as well, particularly when they were being attacked.

The award for most surprising claws goes to Therizinosaurus. This strange Cretaceous dinosaur had claws that resembled large knives. Each claw could grow up to 3 feet long—that's about the size of a human arm! The claws were useful for grabbing leaves and could also be used as weapons to keep predators away.

3 feet

Therizinosaurus

DINOSAUR SKIN

Everything we know about dinosaur skin comes from the few dinosaur fossils we have, which for the most part don't have any skin left on them. Still, oftentimes the imprint of the skin on fossils is enough to give us a few clues.

Finding a skin imprint on a dinosaur fossil is quite rare. Imprints form when the body of a dead dinosaur dehydrates within a particulary dry environment. Before the remains can fully fossilize, minerals infuse the skin and body parts, sometimes leaving imprints.

Dinosaur

Lizard

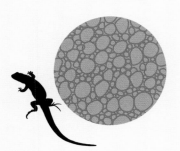

Crocodile

SCALES

Fossils confirm that dinosaurs generally had hard skin covered in scales, which makes them similar to modern-day reptiles. Thus, by observing modern-day reptiles, we can learn a great deal about what dinosaur skin was like. However, not all dinosaurs had the same types of skin and scales. Because dinosaurs were around for millions of years, there was plenty of time for many distinct species to evolve. Even modern reptiles don't all have the same skin type. Lizard skin is much different than crocodile skin, for example.

Edmontosaurus

Edmontosaurus had thick, hard skin that folded along its joints, legs, and neck to allow for movement.

Hadrosaurus

Hadrosaurus had thick skin covered in plates of various sizes.

Psittacosaurus

Psittacosaurus had skin covered in circular scales. One specimen's tail was covered in hollow, bristlelike structures up to 6 inches long, which are similar to the spikes of modern porcupines.

T. rex

T. rex had hard skin covered in rough scales and spots.

PLUMAGE

Paleontologists have known about the close evolutionary relationship between dinosaurs and birds for over 150 years thanks to the remains of a small, feathered reptile called Archaeopteryx. But it was only in the 1990s that the discovery of an incredibly fossil-rich site changed our view of these animals forever. The remains found at the site belonged to peculiar dinosaurs with features similar to modern-day feathers and plumes.

Today we know that many dinosaurs were warm-blooded, like birds and mammals. Scales weren't very useful for maintaining heat, so some dinosaurs developed feathers or plumes to help keep their bodies warm.

Because scales are not suitable for such a function, these animals evolved structures as soft as fur: plumages.

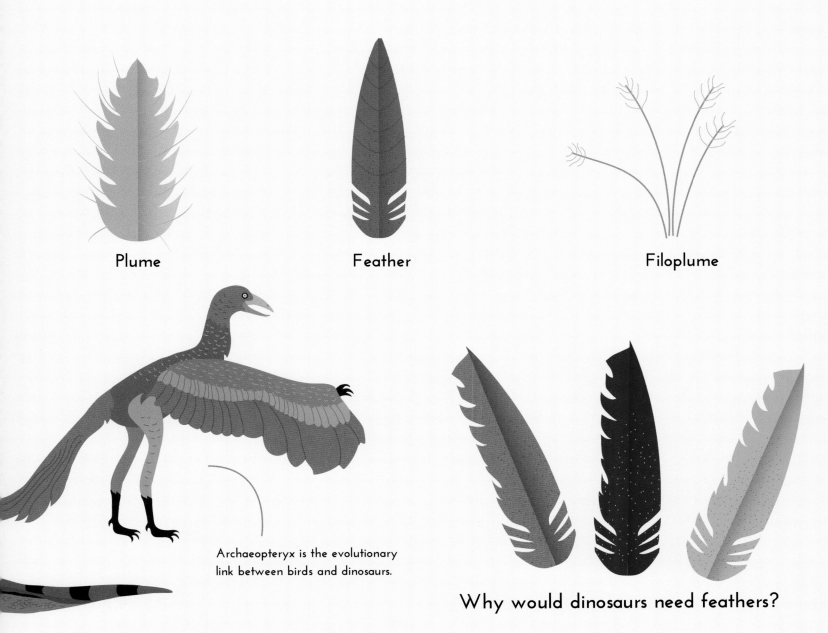

Plume

Feather

Filoplume

Archaeopteryx is the evolutionary link between birds and dinosaurs.

Later on in the Mesozoic era, plumes evolved into feathers and allowed creatures to fly. Feathers are light and flexible but still very strong and resistant. This makes them perfect for supporting body weight during flight.

Today, scientists know that dinosaurs with plumage appeared around the mid-Mesozoic era.

By the following period, almost all theropods had plumage except for larger species, such as T. rex, which may have had plumes at birth. It's likely that T. rex lost its plumes while growing into adulthood. Can you imagine a T. rex with feathers?

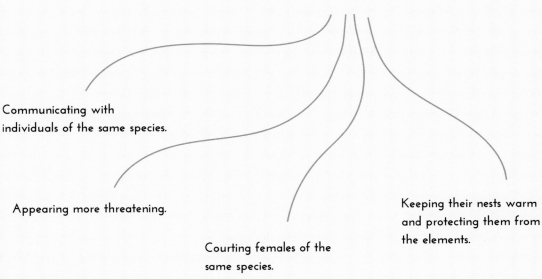

Why would dinosaurs need feathers?

Communicating with individuals of the same species.

Appearing more threatening.

Courting females of the same species.

Keeping their nests warm and protecting them from the elements.

COLORS

Unfortunately we don't know much about dinosaur colors. The pigments responsible for skin color haven't been preserved in dinosaur fossil imprints or dehydrated dinosaur skin. Many paleontologists believe that dinosaurs—much like modern reptiles—used the colors and patterns of their skins to blend into their environments and avoid detection by predators or prey.

It's possible there were brightly colored dinosaurs, much like reptiles such as chameleons or lizards. The bright and vivid colors probably helped certain dinosaurs attract mates or send social signals to other members of their species.

What was dinosaur skin useful for?

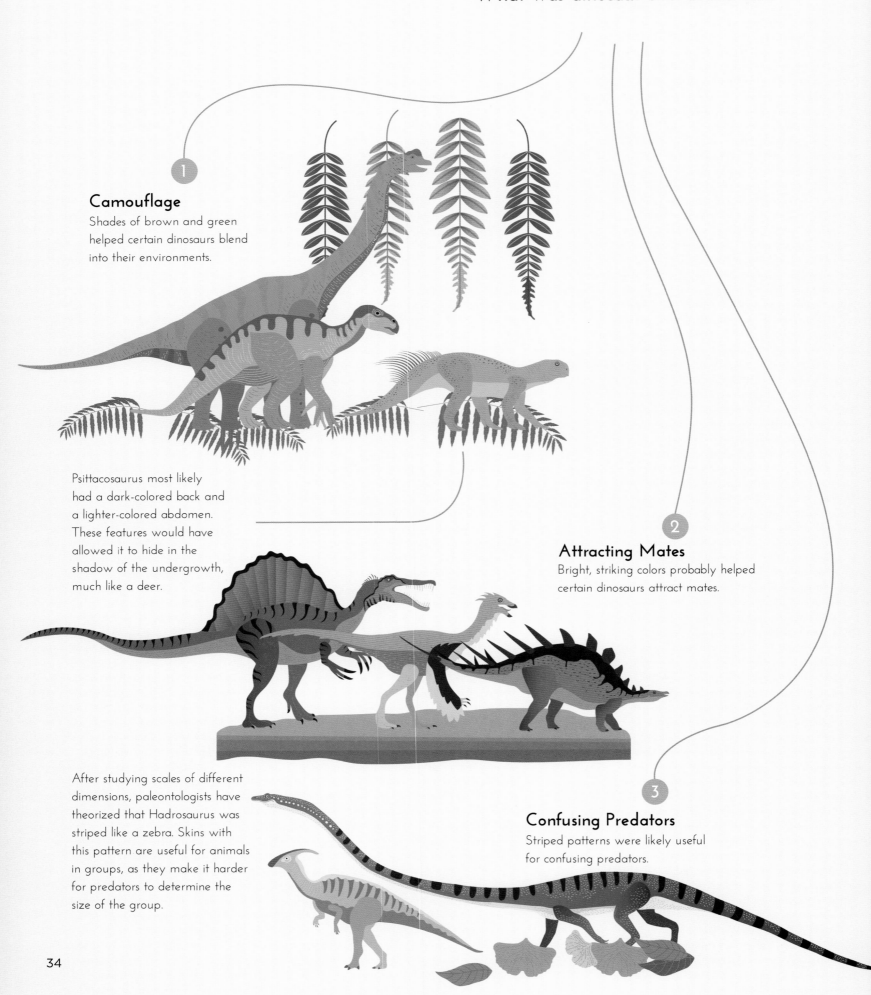

1 Camouflage
Shades of brown and green helped certain dinosaurs blend into their environments.

Psittacosaurus most likely had a dark-colored back and a lighter-colored abdomen. These features would have allowed it to hide in the shadow of the undergrowth, much like a deer.

2 Attracting Mates
Bright, striking colors probably helped certain dinosaurs attract mates.

After studying scales of different dimensions, paleontologists have theorized that Hadrosaurus was striped like a zebra. Skins with this pattern are useful for animals in groups, as they make it harder for predators to determine the size of the group.

3 Confusing Predators
Striped patterns were likely useful for confusing predators.

PLUMES

Plumes are a different matter. Inside fossilized dinosaur plumes, scientists have found melanosomes, which are tiny structures responsible for giving plumes their colors.

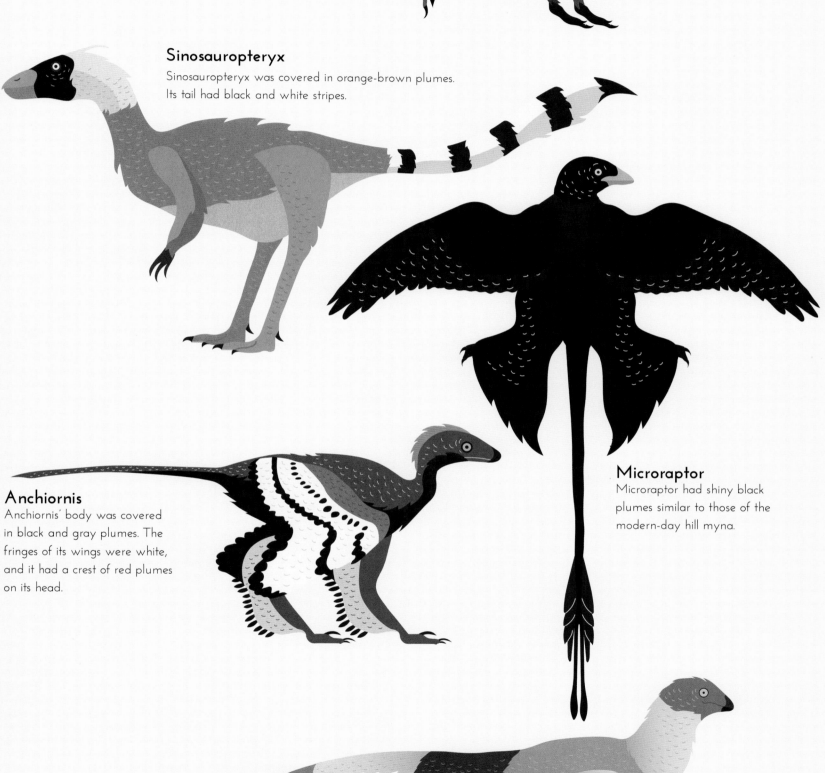

Yi qi
Yi qi had mostly black plumage. Its head featured yellow and brown plumes.

Sinosauropteryx
Sinosauropteryx was covered in orange-brown plumes. Its tail had black and white stripes.

Microraptor
Microraptor had shiny black plumes similar to those of the modern-day hill myna.

Anchiornis
Anchiornis' body was covered in black and gray plumes. The fringes of its wings were white, and it had a crest of red plumes on its head.

Serikornis
Serikornis' plumage alternated between light and dark sections along its wings and tail.

TWO LEGS OR FOUR?

Although it's impossible for us to observe dinosaurs walking, we can imagine their walking speeds and movements by observing fossils of their feet and footprints preserved inside layers of rock.

Unlike modern reptiles, dinosaurs often had very long legs. This was especially true of dinosaurs known to be fast runners, such as the theropods and the ornithopods. The gigantic sauropods had sturdy legs to support their heavy bodies.

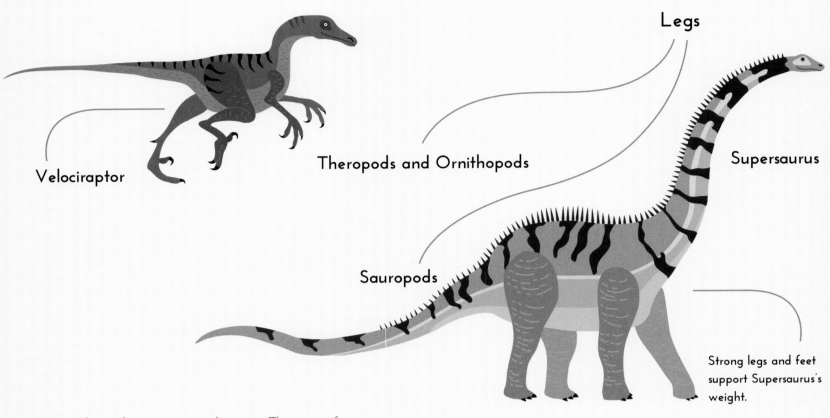

Legs

Velociraptor

Theropods and Ornithopods

Sauropods

Supersaurus

Strong legs and feet support Supersaurus's weight.

We need to make an important distinction. There were four-legged dinosaurs, which walked using all four legs, and two-legged dinosaurs, which walked on their two hind legs.

Some species could choose to walk on two legs or four, much like modern-day bears or gorillas.

TWO-LEGGED

Regarding two-legged dinosaurs, their front legs weren't used for movement. These front legs were "prehensile," meaning they were used for tearing leaves or finding prey.

FOUR-LEGGED

Four-legged dinosaurs often had front legs that were shorter than their rear legs. Some could lift up the front parts of their bodies for a short period using their back legs, but when it came to running, they used all four legs.

T. rex

Tarbosaurus

Large predators like T. rex and the Tarbosaurus had legs that were tiny compared to the rest of their bodies.

Theropods

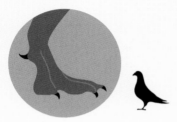

Theropods had feet similar to those of birds, with three toes pointed straight ahead and a small claw facing backward.

Sauropods

Sauropods' feet were padded to help absorb the force of their heavy steps.

Hadrosaurus

Hadrosaurus' toes had fleshy pads between them that would expand upon touching the ground, similar to camels' feet.

CLAWS

Carnivores often had sharp, bladelike claws on the ends of their feet, while plant-eaters like Triceratops and Hadrosaurus had claws that were more like hooves.

Predators called "raptors" had feet with clawed toes. Usually one toe was much sharper and pointier than the others. When walking, raptors would keep this larger toe raised so as not to hurt it. They used this toe as a blade when hunting other prey.

The daggerlike claws of Velociraptor.

3 feet
Therizinosaurus

0.78 feet
Utahraptor

0.65 feet
Giant armadillo

And what about modern animals?

3.5 inches
Velociraptor

4 inches
Siberian tiger

3.5 inches

Sloth

4 inches
T. rex

Golden eagle

2.5 inches

FOOTPRINTS

We can learn a lot about dinosaurs by studying their footprints. The prints show us the anatomy and shape of the given dinosaur's foot, which can tell us whether they were a carnivore or a herbivore.

Sauropods

Ceratopsidae

Ankylosaurus

DINOSAUR SPEED

Dinosaur speeds can be estimated with the help of a little math. Paleontologists only need the length of the dinosaur's step and the approximate length of its leg in order to calculate its speed.

One of the fastest dinosaurs was Ornithomimus, which could reach speeds of up to 40 miles per hour. That's about as fast as an ostrich can run. Scientists found Ornithomimus footprints that were almost 9 feet away from each other!

Theropods
They left trident-shape footprints.

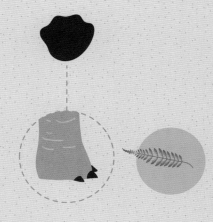

Sauropods
They left large holes in the ground.

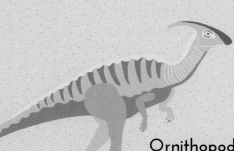

Ornithopoda

Small Theropods

Big Theropods

Sequences of footprints form a trail. Trails are useful because they tell us about the animal's gait. Footprints positioned closer together mean a faster gait. Footprints farther away mean a slower gait.

The more distant dinosaur footprints are from each other, the more likely it is that the dinosaur was walking when it made them. The prints can also tell us how big the dinosaur was and whether it walked on two legs or four.

HOW A FOSSIL FOOTPRINT FORMS

Dinosaurs left footprints on muddy grounds, which then dried up and hardened. Later they were covered up by layers of sediment that became rock. This process is how paleontologists have been able to discover so many dinosaur footprints even though dinosaurs went extinct millions of years ago.

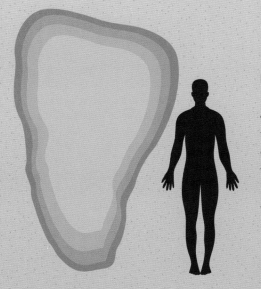

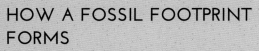

Dinosaur footprints found in northwestern Australia in 2017 are among the biggest ever discovered. At the site, the largest tracks belonged to sauropods. Scientists also discovered tracks from about four different types of ornithopod dinosaurs (two-legged herbivores) and about six different types of armored dinosaurs, including Stegosaurus.

BABY DINOSAURS:
NESTS, EGGS, AND HATCHLINGS

EGGS

Like reptiles and birds, dinosaurs reproduced by laying eggs. The size, shape, and number naturally depended on the species. The characteristics of the eggs, such as their shape and shell structure, help paleontologists determine whether they were laid by theropods, sauropods, or some other kind of dinosaur.

Female dinosaurs could lay up to 20 eggs at a time. Many were eaten by predators before hatching.

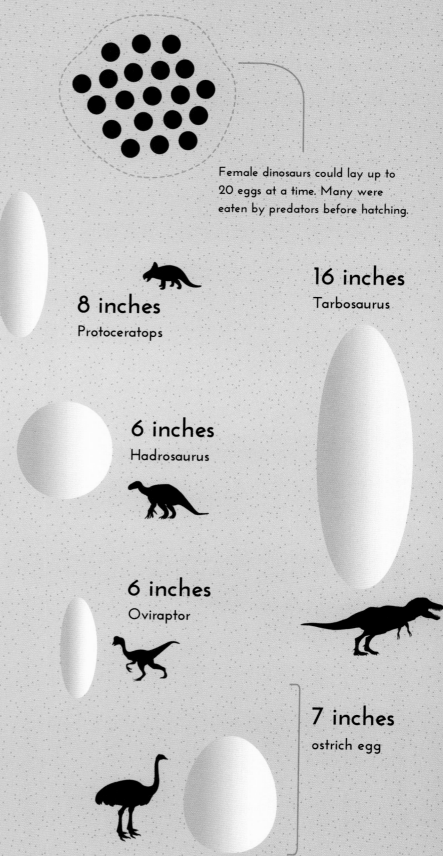

8 inches
Protoceratops

16 inches
Tarbosaurus

8.4 inches
Titanosaurus

6 inches
Hadrosaurus

6 inches
Oviraptor

7 inches
ostrich egg

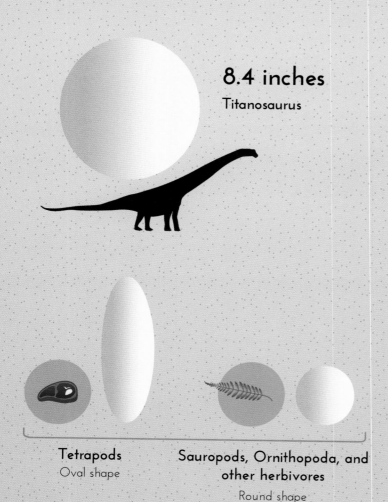

Tetrapods
Oval shape

Sauropods, Ornithopoda, and other herbivores
Round shape

SHAPE AND SIZE

The shape of the dinosaur egg can tell us a little about the dinosaur's preferred environment. For example, oval eggs were taller and could fit into narrower spaces. Plus, since they were oval, they didn't roll as easily, so they could be laid on hills or inclines.

Paleontologists can say confidently that no dinosaur egg has ever been longer than 23 inches. Bigger eggs require thicker shells, but the shells still need to allow oxygen to enter, so they can't be too thick. Therefore, 23 inches appears to be the limit. If the egg were any larger, it would be too thick for the embryo to receive the oxygen it needs.

SHELL THICKNESS

The thickest shell ever found was 0.2 inch thick. Its surface had tiny holes that would have allowed the embryo to breathe. They likely also ensured that the humidity levels within the egg were comfortable for the embryo. The number of holes in the egg is specific to each species, so paleontologists can use this information to determine which dinosaur laid the eggs in question.

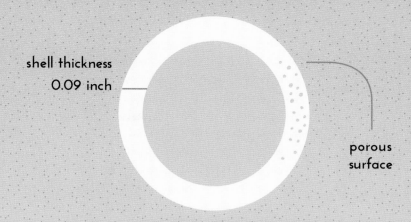

shell thickness
0.09 inch

porous surface

eggs with few holes
laid on the surface

19 inches
Segnosaurus

very porous eggs
laid underground

Most dinosaur eggs have been found in China, Mongolia, Argentina, India, and North America.

COLOR

We don't know exactly what color dinosaur eggs were. Recent studies from Yale University have shown that many modern species, like birds, lay eggs with colors similar to those of their surroundings, perhaps to help hide them from predators. Therefore it's possible that dinosaur eggs laid underground were white or gray, while the ones laid aboveground had different colors depending on the location.

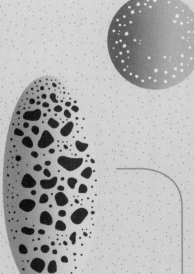

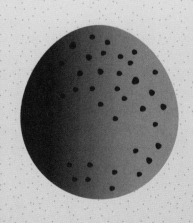

Eggs with patches or spots may have been easier to hide in certain environments.

Eggs from the dinosaur species Heyuannia were apparently blue, much like the eggs of modern-day emus and cassowaries.

NESTS

Each species of dinosaur laid its eggs in a different way. Some laid them in spirals, some in rows, and some in no pattern at all. However, all dinosaurs laid their eggs inside nests.

Some dinosaur species would place plants on top of their nests to help keep the eggs warm until they hatched.

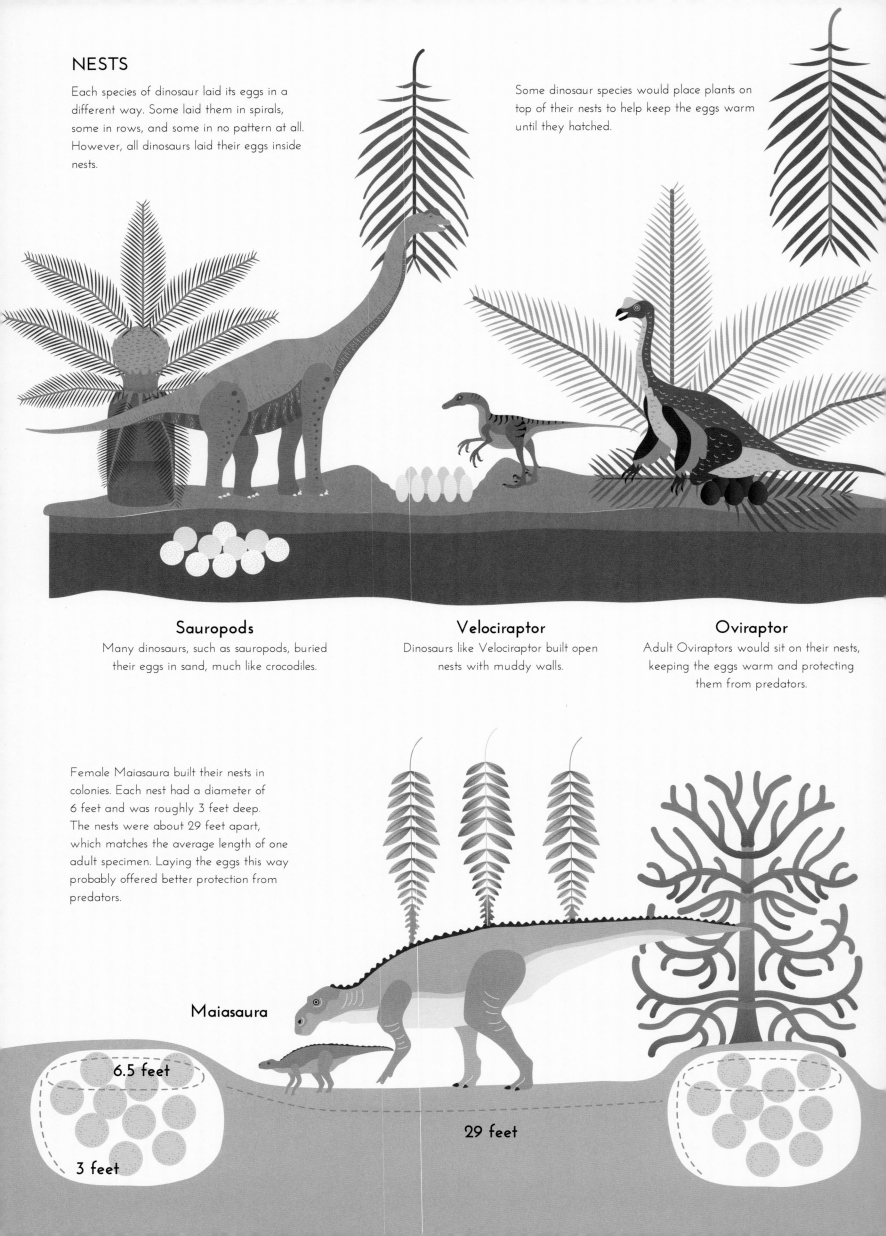

Sauropods
Many dinosaurs, such as sauropods, buried their eggs in sand, much like crocodiles.

Velociraptor
Dinosaurs like Velociraptor built open nests with muddy walls.

Oviraptor
Adult Oviraptors would sit on their nests, keeping the eggs warm and protecting them from predators.

Female Maiasaura built their nests in colonies. Each nest had a diameter of 6 feet and was roughly 3 feet deep. The nests were about 29 feet apart, which matches the average length of one adult specimen. Laying the eggs this way probably offered better protection from predators.

Maiasaura

6.5 feet

3 feet

29 feet

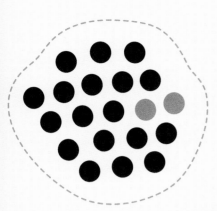

Baby dinosaurs probably had similar survival rates to those of modern reptiles and birds—only 10-15 percent were likely to survive the first year of life.

HATCHLINGS

As is the case with crocodiles and turtles, the gender of the hatchling is influenced by the temperature of the environment. If the weather was hot, more males hatched. If it was colder, there were probably more females. After leaving the egg, babies had to quickly learn how to find food and survive.

The remains of baby Troodon specimens show that, at birth, they were probably already able to walk and may have even been strong enough to leave the nest, much like baby ducklings.

Specimens of Hadrosaurus babies show partially developed teeth, but their legs weren't quite developed enough to allow them to roam around. Therefore it's very likely that Hadrosaurus adults took care of the babies during their first few weeks, bringing them food and possibly even chewing it for them.

A mother sauropod was 2,500 times bigger than her hatchlings.

The growth process of a sauropod is pretty impressive. When hatching, a baby sauropod generally weighed less than 11 pounds. Within 30 years, they would grow 10,000 times heavier than this original weight. This kind of growth rate has never been observed in any other being on Earth, extinct or alive.

JOINING THE GROUP:
PACKS, HERDS, AND FLOCKS

WHY LIVE AS A GROUP?

Not all dinosaurs lived alone—quite the opposite! Several fossil sites have shown that many species lived in groups. In these sites, numerous examples of the same species have been discovered. We can infer that entire herds died around the same time, possibly surprised by a cataclysmic event such as an earthquake, a sandstorm, or a volcanic eruption.

HERDS

In some fossil sites, footprints left by several dinosaurs have been discovered in close proximity. Many plant-eaters lived and moved in herds, finding food and perhaps even nesting together. The big advantage of forming a herd was that it made it harder for predators to attack.

Some herds might have been only temporary, possibly formed by dinosaurs who only wanted to graze peacefully for a short period within the same area.

Dinosaurs of different species often made long seasonal migrations together in order to safely seek out food in another location.

When migrating, smaller dinosaurs walked in the center of the herd to stay protected.

Living in the herd meant doing a lot of walking together, and unfortunately this also meant stepping on feet and tails from time to time, as shown by the broken bones on many dinosaur fossils!

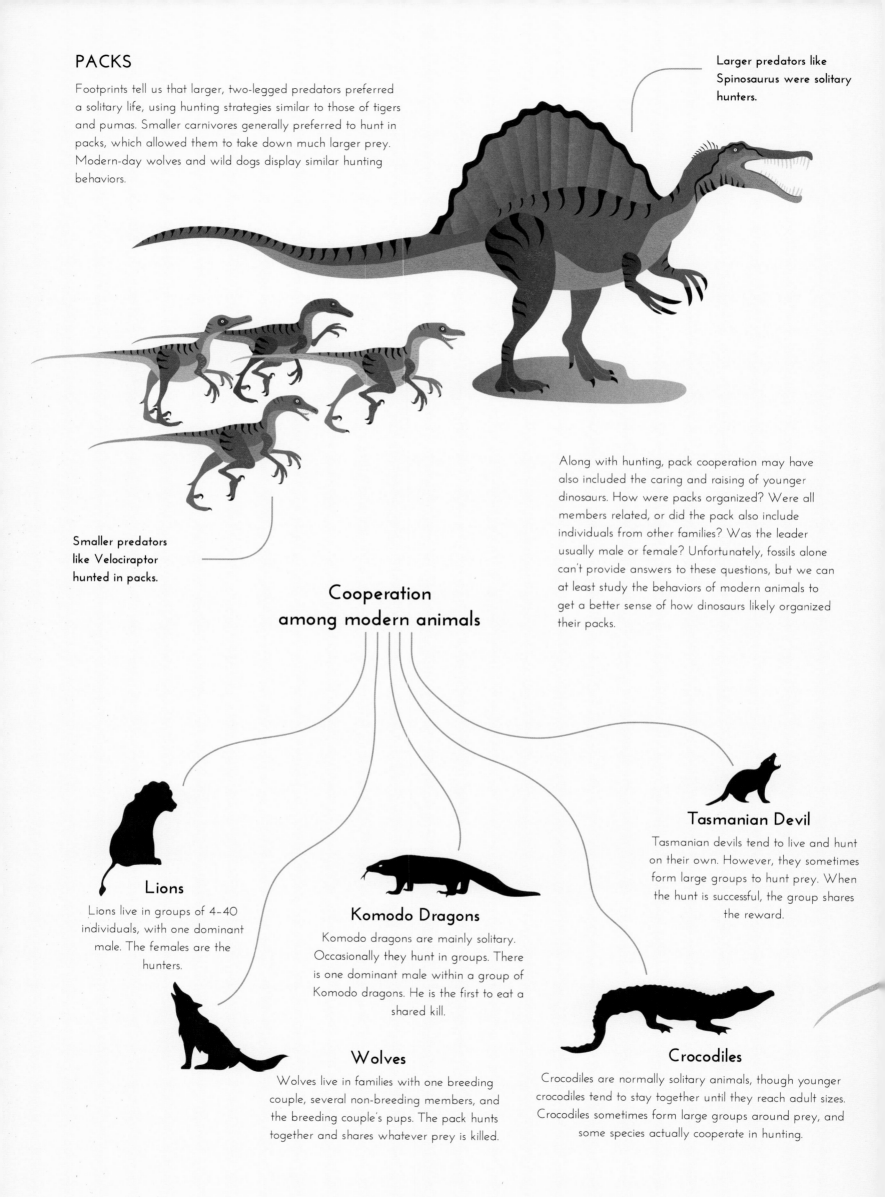

PACKS

Footprints tell us that larger, two-legged predators preferred a solitary life, using hunting strategies similar to those of tigers and pumas. Smaller carnivores generally preferred to hunt in packs, which allowed them to take down much larger prey. Modern-day wolves and wild dogs display similar hunting behaviors.

Larger predators like Spinosaurus were solitary hunters.

Smaller predators like Velociraptor hunted in packs.

Along with hunting, pack cooperation may have also included the caring and raising of younger dinosaurs. How were packs organized? Were all members related, or did the pack also include individuals from other families? Was the leader usually male or female? Unfortunately, fossils alone can't provide answers to these questions, but we can at least study the behaviors of modern animals to get a better sense of how dinosaurs likely organized their packs.

Cooperation among modern animals

Lions

Lions live in groups of 4-40 individuals, with one dominant male. The females are the hunters.

Komodo Dragons

Komodo dragons are mainly solitary. Occasionally they hunt in groups. There is one dominant male within a group of Komodo dragons. He is the first to eat a shared kill.

Wolves

Wolves live in families with one breeding couple, several non-breeding members, and the breeding couple's pups. The pack hunts together and shares whatever prey is killed.

Tasmanian Devil

Tasmanian devils tend to live and hunt on their own. However, they sometimes form large groups to hunt prey. When the hunt is successful, the group shares the reward.

Crocodiles

Crocodiles are normally solitary animals, though younger crocodiles tend to stay together until they reach adult sizes. Crocodiles sometimes form large groups around prey, and some species actually cooperate in hunting.

WHAT DID A DINOSAUR HUNT LOOK LIKE?

Let's imagine a group of dinosaurs hunting prey.

After hours or even days of chasing, a group of small Dromaeosaurus surrounds its now-exhausted prey. The prey could be large or small, but no matter its size, its chances of surviving a group attack would have been minimal. Each individual in the group could bite or swipe with its claws. If one of them got hurt, another could step in to keep up the attack. Slowly but surely, the victim was torn to pieces. Once the prey was sufficiently weakened by its injuries, the group would launch a final attack to finish it off. Then they could eat.

DINOSAUR ROMANCE:
FINDING A PARTNER

In nature, sometimes mating is preceded by a courting ritual. The female is generally approached by one or more males, and she gets to choose which one will be her partner. We don't know for sure if dinosaurs had courting rituals, but paleontologists believe that some species did.

Courting and choosing a partner are essential for the survival of any species. Finding the healthiest and strongest partner is a natural way to increase the chances of having equally healthy offspring that can survive long enough to mate and reproduce.

ACCESSORIZE!

In order to be chosen, the male first had to attract the female's attention. This was easier to accomplish if he had bright colors, big horns, or an attractive crest. Many dinosaur species likely had extravagant colors or special physical characteristics that would have made them look irresistible to females.

Monolophosaurus jiangxi

Monolophosaurus jiangxi was a theropod with an unusual appearance. It lived in Asia about 170 million years ago. The bony crest on its head may have functioned as a kind of flag to help attract the attention of potential mates. The crest may have also served as a sound amplifier involved in communication.

Cryolophosaurus

At the top of Cryolophosaurus's skull sat a distinctive, curly crest. Thin and grooved, the crest is notably similar to the comb Spanish dancers wear on their heads when dancing the flamenco. Because of the fragility of the crest, paleontologists believe the only purpose it could have served was helping to attract mates.

Generally speaking, females didn't have as many distinctive characteristics as males did. This phenomenon is called "sexual dimorphism." Young males didn't typically display physical characteristics used in courting until they were closer to mating age. In terms of actual mating rituals, paleontologists speculate that certain species of carnivorous dinosaurs performed mating dances to try to win the favor of females.

Dilophosaurus

Dilophosaurus had two prominent parallel crests on top of its skull, which were continuations of its nasal and lacrimal bones. Because the crests were very delicate, scientists believe they were used either for courting or to help individuals recognize members of the same species.

MATING FIGHTS

Reproduction also required fending off potential competitors. The easiest way to accomplish this was to scare them away. But if that didn't work, dinosaurs needed to be prepared to show their physical strength. When several males wanted to mate with a female, fights were inevitable. Fights were also used to help establish a hierarchy of strength within a group. The ways opponents challenged each other varied depending on the species. The huge, long-necked male Apatosaurus, for example, would fight in pairs, striking at each other with their long necks and sometimes accidentally wrapping them around each other!

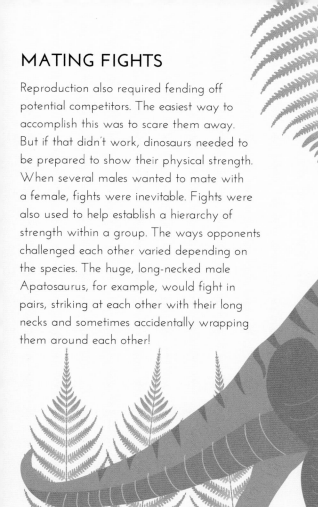

Pachycephalosaurus had a round skull with bony spikes. The top of its skull could be 8 inches thick. Scientists believe such an extra-thick skull came in handy when males head-butted each other to win the favor of females. Modern-day antelope display similar courting behaviors.

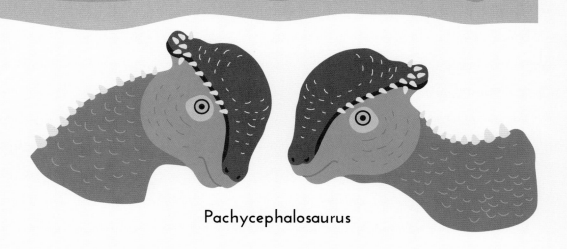

Pachycephalosaurus

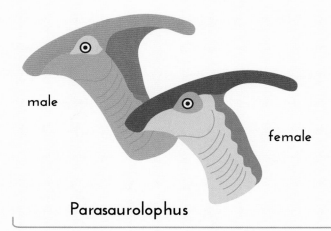

male

female

Parasaurolophus

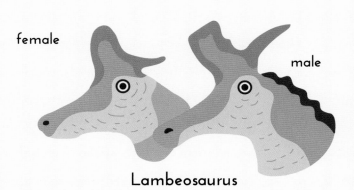

female

male

Lambeosaurus

Parasaurolophus and Lambeosaurus featured distinctive crests in both sexes, though the crests were more developed in the males. Lambeosaurus's crest was pointier and more prominent, while Lambeosaurus's crest extended farther behind its head. Crests could be intimidating to other males. Additionally, because they were hollow, they may have also helped to amplify their sounds and calls.

TAKING OFF:
THE EVOLUTION OF BIRDS

Today we consider it a given that birds are direct descendants of carnivorous dinosaurs. Crocodiles are more closely related to dinosaurs than birds, so scientists tend to think of them almost like dinosaur cousins.

A COMMON ANCESTOR

When we look closely at modern-day birds, we notice that they actually share many characteristics with dinosaurs, or at least with the two-legged carnivorous dinosaurs that had plumage.

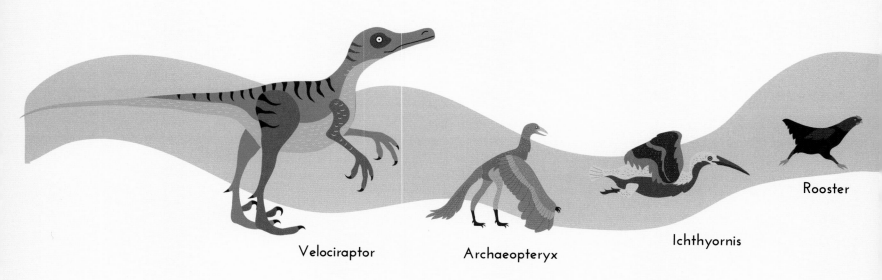

Velociraptor

Archaeopteryx

Ichthyornis

Rooster

The oldest birdlike dinosaur that we know of is Archaeopteryx, which dates back to the late Jurassic period (about 150 million years ago). It was about as big as a modern-day pheasant. Its teeth and long, bony tail made it look very similar to another small dinosaur from the same period, Compsognathus, except that Archaeopteryx's tail had plumage and Compsognathus's didn't.

Birds are considered descendants of theropods, which were two-legged dinosaurs that fed mainly on meat.

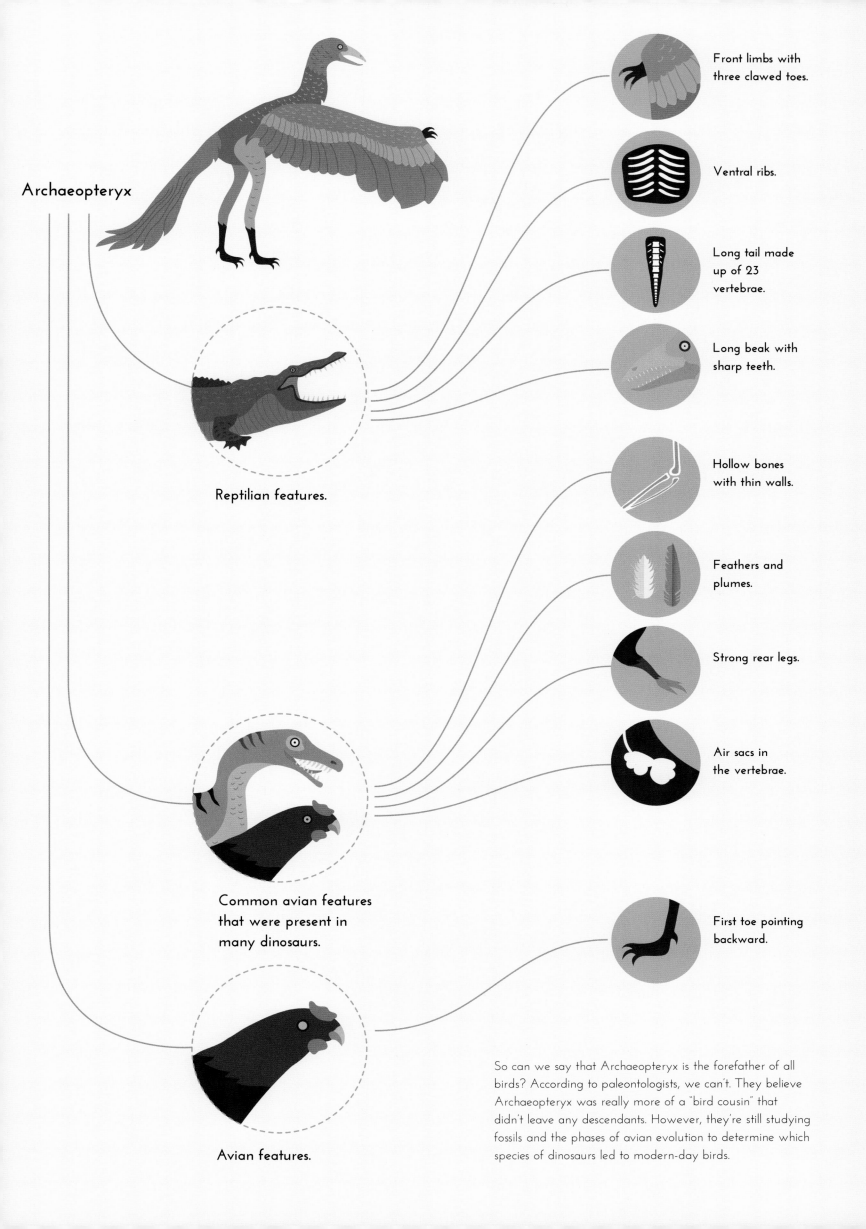

Archaeopteryx

Front limbs with three clawed toes.

Ventral ribs.

Long tail made up of 23 vertebrae.

Long beak with sharp teeth.

Reptilian features.

Hollow bones with thin walls.

Feathers and plumes.

Strong rear legs.

Air sacs in the vertebrae.

Common avian features that were present in many dinosaurs.

First toe pointing backward.

So can we say that Archaeopteryx is the forefather of all birds? According to paleontologists, we can't. They believe Archaeopteryx was really more of a "bird cousin" that didn't leave any descendants. However, they're still studying fossils and the phases of avian evolution to determine which species of dinosaurs led to modern-day birds.

Avian features.

HOW DID BIRDS LEARN TO FLY?

Paleontologists are still struggling to answer the above question. We know that many smaller species of theropods had front legs covered in plumes. These species could also glide short distances, allowing themselves to be carried by the air without expending any energy themselves, but they couldn't actively fly just yet.

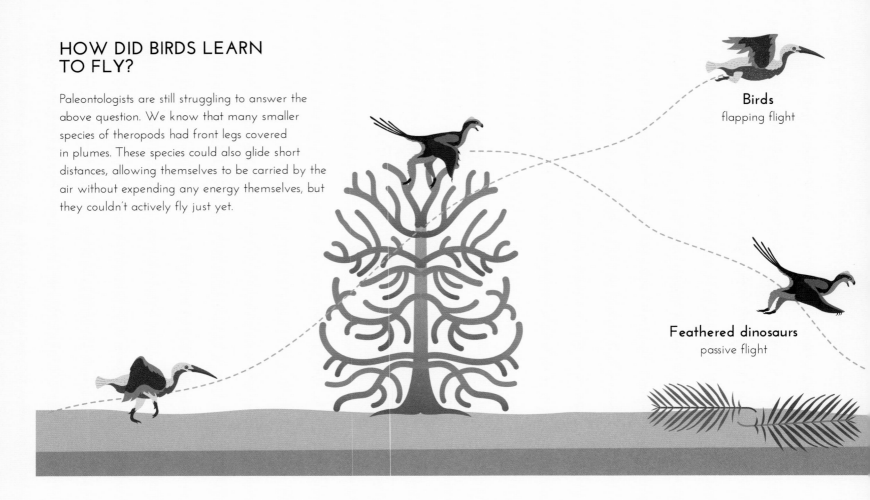

Birds
flapping flight

Feathered dinosaurs
passive flight

Most modern-day birds perform something called "flapping flight," which requires lots of energy and wings that can complete many delicate motions with incredible speed. It took millions of years of evolution for bird wings to gain the ability to actively fly.

To take off and fly, birds need:

A relatively small, light body.

Big wings.

Highly developed chest muscles and sternum.

Powerul leg muscles.

It's still not completely clear how flight developed in animals. There are two main theories: the arboreal theory and the terrestrial theory. Supporters of the arboreal theory believe that the ancestors of modern birds leapt from branch to branch, eventually evolving from gliding flight to fully flapping flight.

The terrestrial theory states that running and jumping eventually led to flying. Animals may have evolved to have wings for stability purposes while running at high speeds. Flying would thus have resulted from animals with wings learning to jump higher and higher with the help of their wings.

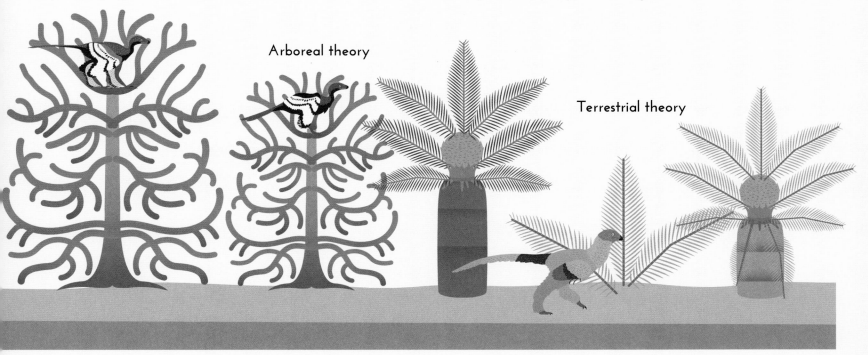

Arboreal theory

Terrestrial theory

The evolution from dinosaurs to birds required many small transformations along the way:

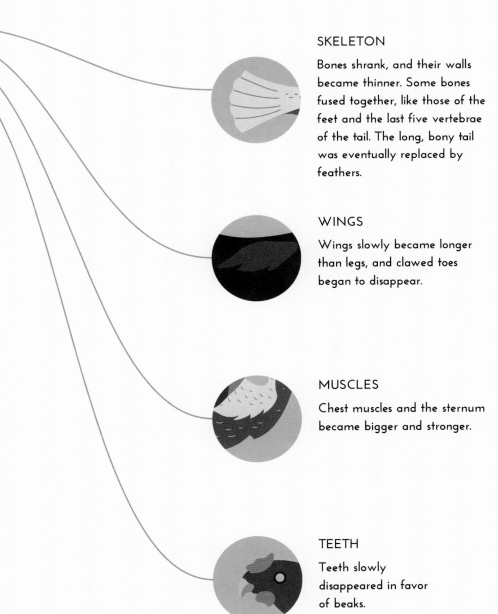

SKELETON

Bones shrank, and their walls became thinner. Some bones fused together, like those of the feet and the last five vertebrae of the tail. The long, bony tail was eventually replaced by feathers.

WINGS

Wings slowly became longer than legs, and clawed toes began to disappear.

MUSCLES

Chest muscles and the sternum became bigger and stronger.

TEETH

Teeth slowly disappeared in favor of beaks.

WHO WAS THE FOREFATHER OF MODERN BIRDS?

We don't know the answer to this question yet. Paleontologists believe it must have been quite small and likely very fast in reproducing. These characteristics would have helped it survive the mass extinction that hit Earth 65 million years ago. Two main groups of birds originated from this ancestor.

After that, birds continued to evolve and diversify for millions of years, eventually becoming the birds we see today. The world now hosts over 10,000 species of birds, and they can still be divided into two main groups: Palaeognathae, which includes flightless birds such as ostriches, kiwis, emus, and rheas, and Neognathae, which includes all other birds.

LORDS OF THE SKY:
PTEROSAURS

In the era of dinosaurs, the sky was populated by flying reptiles called pterosaurs. They varied in size and behavior, but almost all of them had the same basic body structure.

pterosaurs

dinosaurs

230 mya

210 mya

190 mya

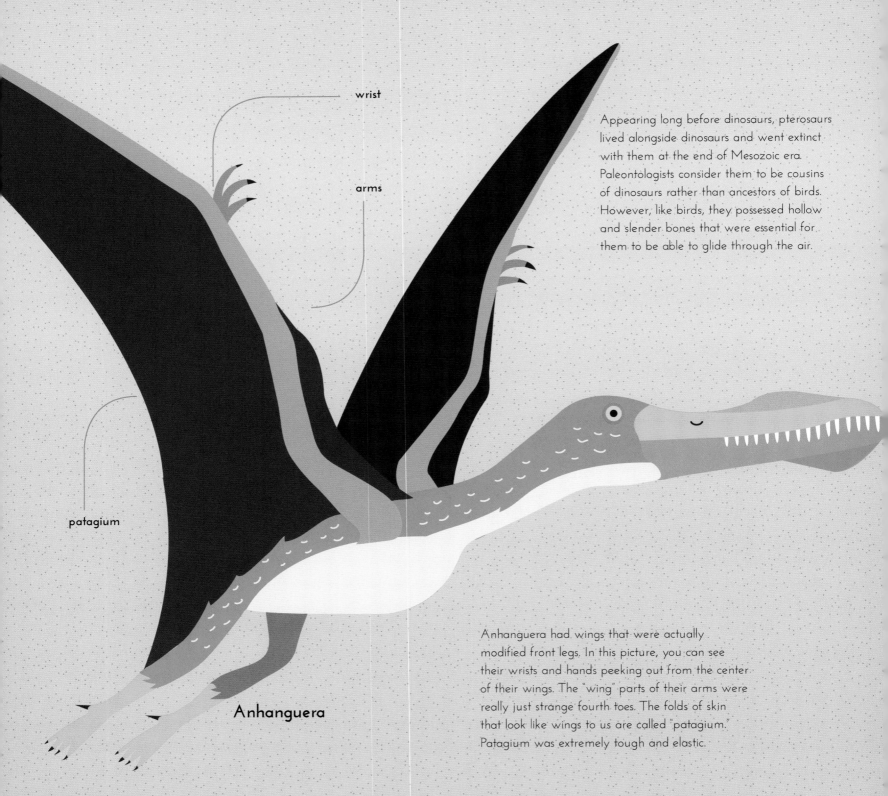

wrist

arms

patagium

Anhanguera

Appearing long before dinosaurs, pterosaurs lived alongside dinosaurs and went extinct with them at the end of Mesozoic era. Paleontologists consider them to be cousins of dinosaurs rather than ancestors of birds. However, like birds, they possessed hollow and slender bones that were essential for them to be able to glide through the air.

Anhanguera had wings that were actually modified front legs. In this picture, you can see their wrists and hands peeking out from the center of their wings. The "wing" parts of their arms were really just strange fourth toes. The folds of skin that look like wings to us are called "patagium." Patagium was extremely tough and elastic.

The sizes of pterosaurs varied considerably. Quetzalcoatlus northropi holds the record for the largest one. No past or present bird has ever come close to being as large as Quetzalcoatlus northropi was!

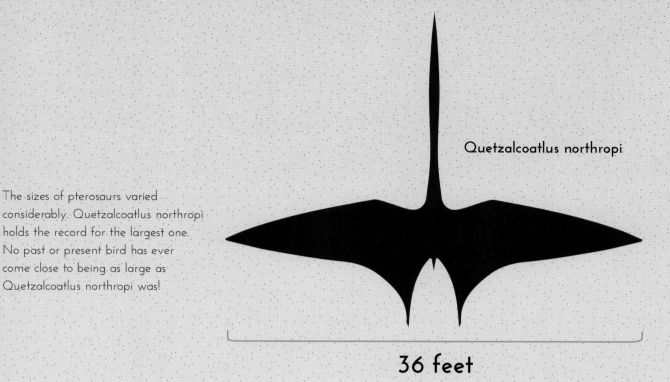

Quetzalcoatlus northropi

36 feet

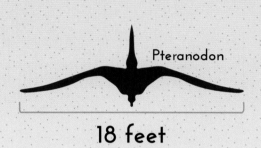

Pteranodon

18 feet

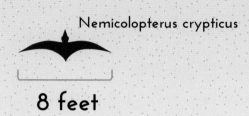

Nemicolopterus crypticus

8 feet

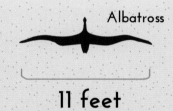

Albatross

11 feet

Golden eagle

7.5 feet

BIRDS AND PTEROSAURS

Check out the main differences between birds and pterosaurs.

1

WING

Pterosaurs' wings resemble bat wings.

2

PLUMAGE

Pterosaurs had no plumage.

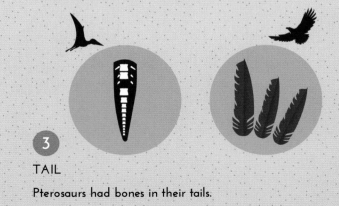

3

TAIL

Pterosaurs had bones in their tails.

FLYING THROUGH THE AIR

Just like bird wings, the shape of dinosaur wings can tell us a lot about the type of flight the creature was capable of.

Pteranodon longiceps

Short, wide wings were handy for changing direction quickly while escaping predators.

Nemicolopterus crypticus

Long, slender wings were better for flying longer distances.

Quetzalcoatlus northropi

COULD FLYING DINOSAURS ALSO RUN?

All pterosaurs could fly, but could they also run on the ground? The short answer is yes. Some species, such as Dimorphodon, developed strong legs. Dimorphodon could run quickly on its rear legs by standing on the tips of its toes. It could also run on four legs if it wanted, leaning on the exposed toes of its wings and closing them like tiny umbrellas.

Other pterosaurs didn't rely so much on walking or running, which was of course clumsier for them (and naturally more tiresome) than flying. Some species hardly traveled on the ground at all, instead using the toes on their wings to hang upside down from tree branches, much like modern-day bats.

9 feet

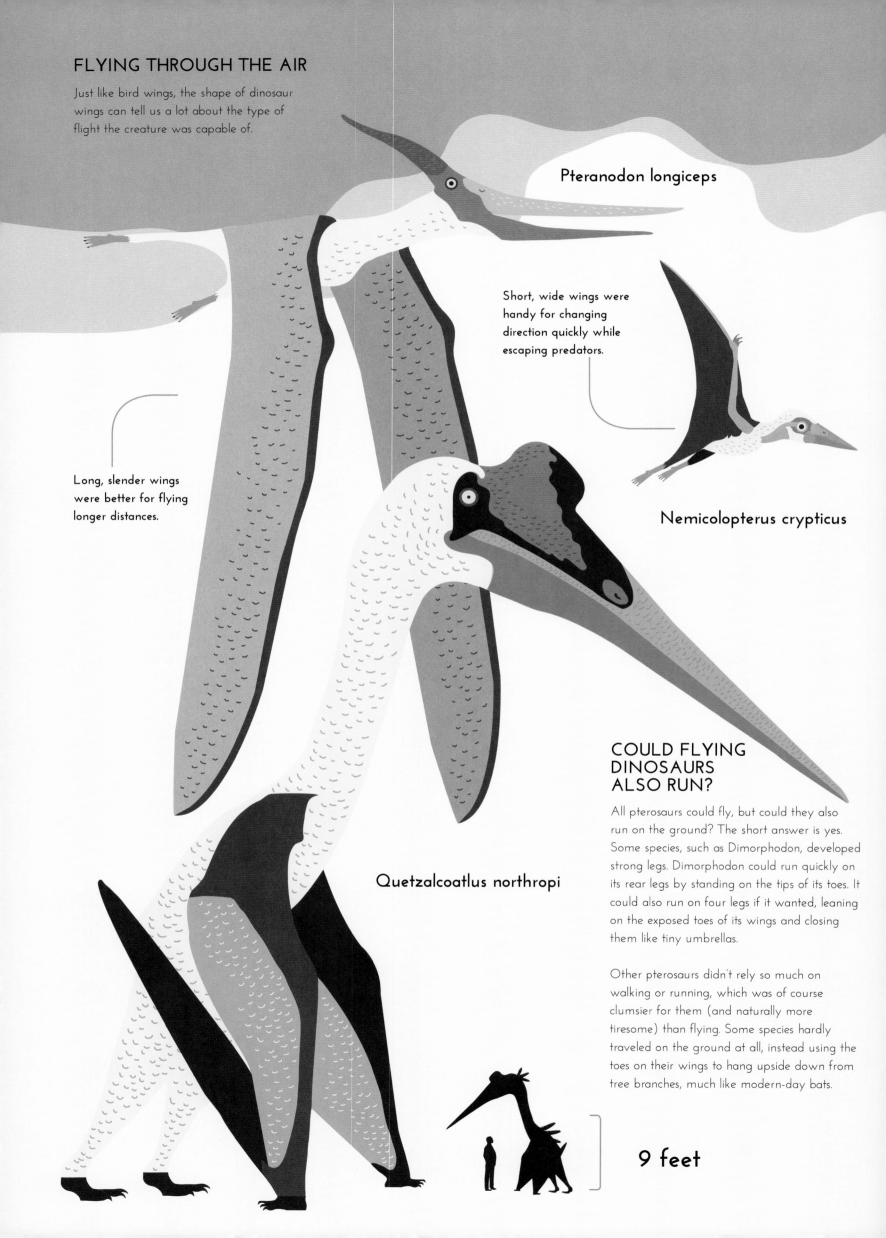

WHAT DID PTEROSAURS EAT?

Many pterosaurs had thick beaks equipped with lots of teeth, but these teeth could be many different sizes and shapes depending on what the given pterosaur's diet was.

long, jagged teeth
fish, insects, and other reptiles

big teeth
mollusks and crustaceans

long, thin teeth that look like they belong to a brush
fish, insects, and other reptiles

toothless
fish

CRESTS

Lots of pterosaurs had crests on their heads, which came in many different colors, shapes, and sizes. They functioned as a way for members of the same species to tell each other apart and to help males attract females. Larger crests were sometimes used to help balance out the weight of larger beaks during flight. Pteranodon is an example of this. Shorter crests may have been used to help pterosaurs steer themselves through the air while flying.

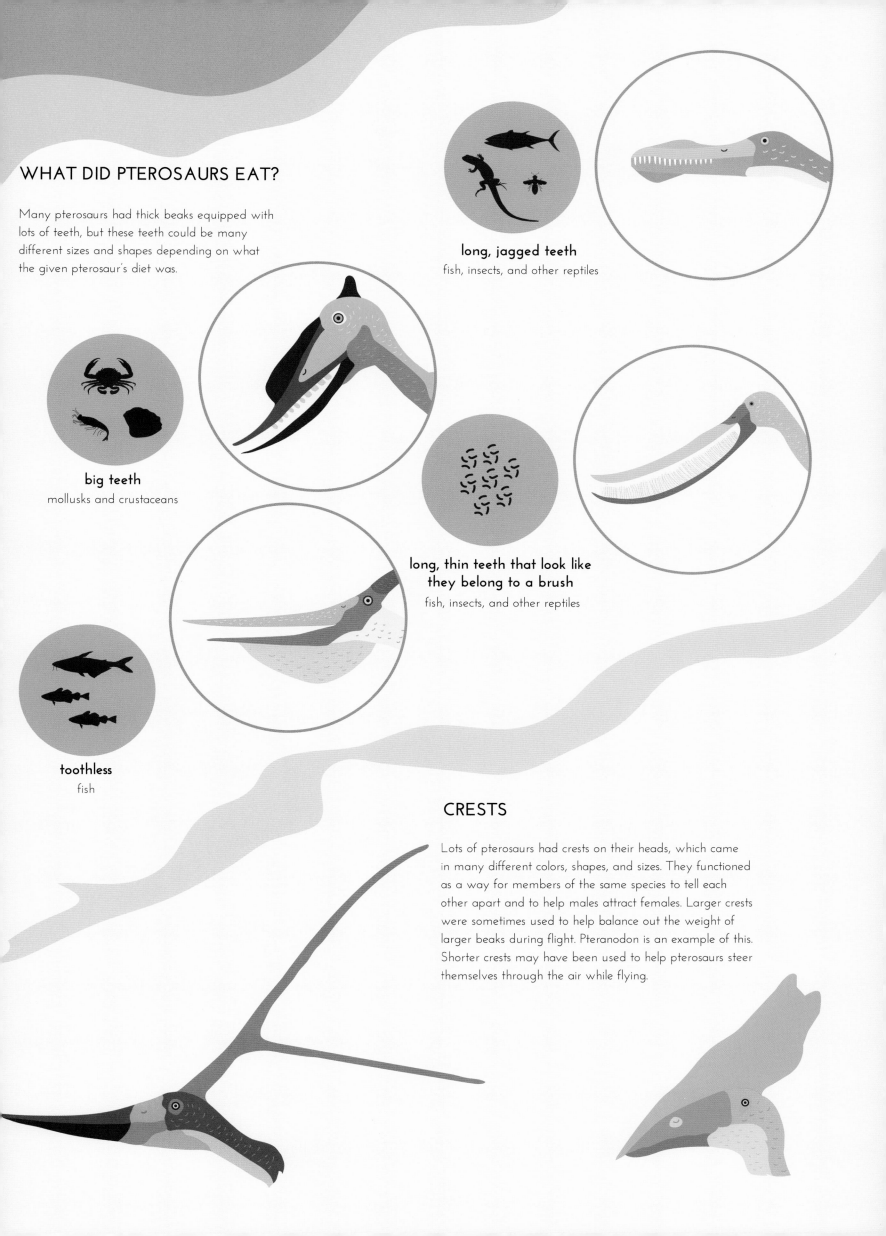

MORE PTEROSAURS

The number of pterosaur species discovered so far is 150, but scientists believe there are thousands more just waiting to be discovered.

PTEROSAURS
known species

150

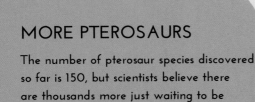

Late Triassic

Jurassic

short wings.

RHAMPHORHYNCHUS

lived around 150 million years ago

short limbs and neck.

long, bony tail with a diamond-shaped rudder on the end.

sharp teeth.

STAYING WARM

Some pterosaur remains feature traces of thin hair, which may have covered their whole bodies. Paleontologists have theorized that pterosaurs were in fact warm-blooded, like birds and mammals. If they were indeed warm-blooded, they would have needed the hair to help protect themselves from the cold.

BORN TO FLY

Unlike dinosaurs, pterosaurs laid soft-shelled eggs. This is why pterosaur egg remains are so hard to come by. At birth, hatchlings likely already had a completely formed set of wings. Paleontologists initially imagined that pterosaur parents were caring and attentive toward their offspring, but today they believe that the young ones became independent immediately after birth.

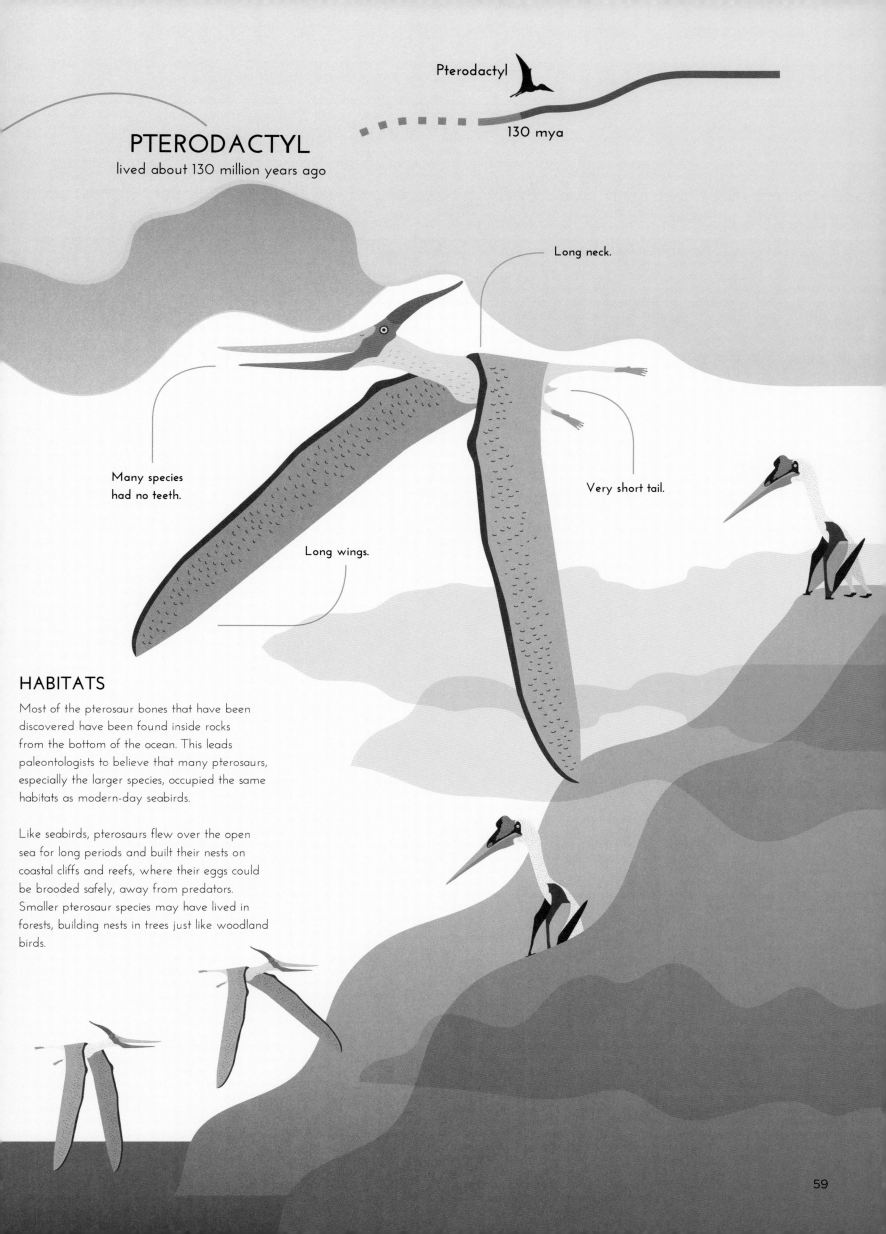

PTERODACTYL
lived about 130 million years ago

Pterodactyl

130 mya

Long neck.

Many species
had no teeth.

Very short tail.

Long wings.

HABITATS

Most of the pterosaur bones that have been
discovered have been found inside rocks
from the bottom of the ocean. This leads
paleontologists to believe that many pterosaurs,
especially the larger species, occupied the same
habitats as modern-day seabirds.

Like seabirds, pterosaurs flew over the open
sea for long periods and built their nests on
coastal cliffs and reefs, where their eggs could
be brooded safely, away from predators.
Smaller pterosaur species may have lived in
forests, building nests in trees just like woodland
birds.

LIVING UNDERWATER:
MARINE REPTILES

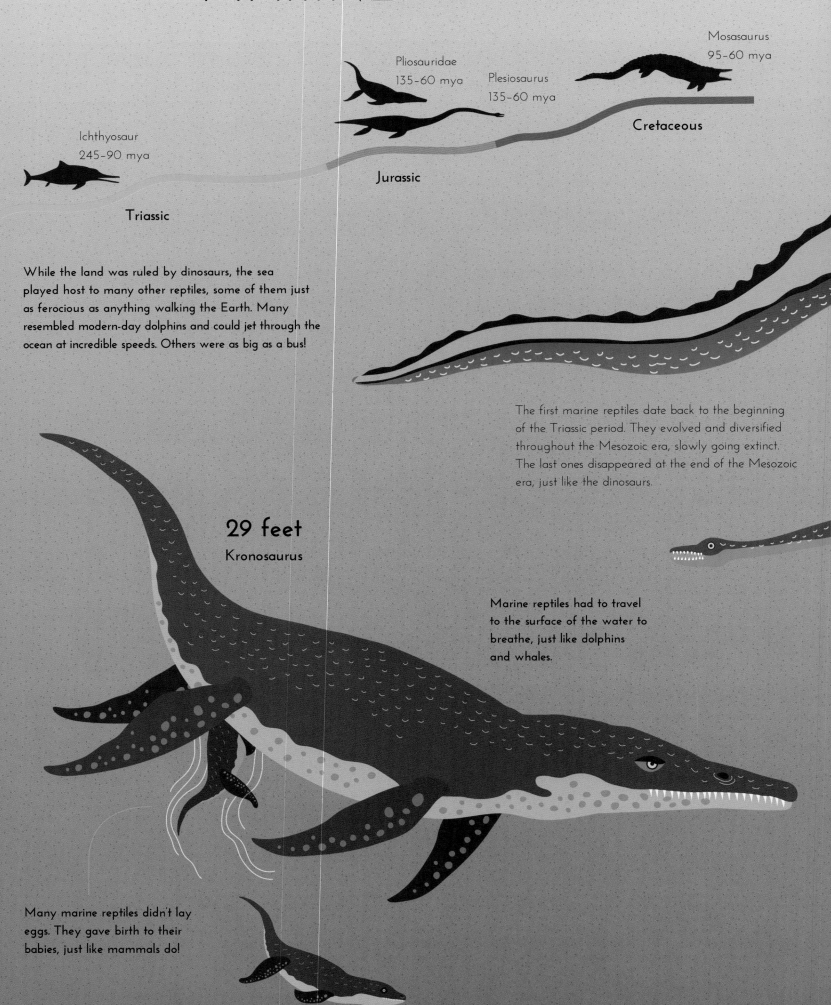

Pliosauridae
135-60 mya

Mosasaurus
95-60 mya

Plesiosaurus
135-60 mya

Cretaceous

Ichthyosaur
245-90 mya

Jurassic

Triassic

While the land was ruled by dinosaurs, the sea played host to many other reptiles, some of them just as ferocious as anything walking the Earth. Many resembled modern-day dolphins and could jet through the ocean at incredible speeds. Others were as big as a bus!

The first marine reptiles date back to the beginning of the Triassic period. They evolved and diversified throughout the Mesozoic era, slowly going extinct. The last ones disappeared at the end of the Mesozoic era, just like the dinosaurs.

29 feet
Kronosaurus

Marine reptiles had to travel to the surface of the water to breathe, just like dolphins and whales.

Many marine reptiles didn't lay eggs. They gave birth to their babies, just like mammals do!

MARINE REPTILE EVOLUTION

In order to move swiftly through the water, marine reptile bodies had to be sleek and hydrodynamic. Over millions of years, reptilian legs evolved into fins and tails, which allowed them to swim with greater speed and control. Ichthyosaurs had pointed snouts armed with tiny, razor-sharp teeth perfect for preying on fish. They propelled themselves forward with a powerful tail that could also shoot them to the surface quickly when they needed to breathe.

19 feet
Ophthalmosaurus

56 feet
Mosasaurus

46 feet
Elasmosaurus

69 feet
Shonisaurus sikanniensis

MOVING UNDERWATER

Fins are the result of millions of years of evolution. Marine reptile ancestors started with five toes. Over time, the number of toes slowly increased as reptiles adapted to the water. Eventually their toes grew connective webbing and became paddles and fins, which made swimming through the water more efficient. Marine reptiles like Pliosaurus had rear fins that were much larger than their frontal fins. Paleontologists believe that many marine reptiles were extremely fast and could reach speeds of up to 40 miles per hour—much like modern-day tuna!

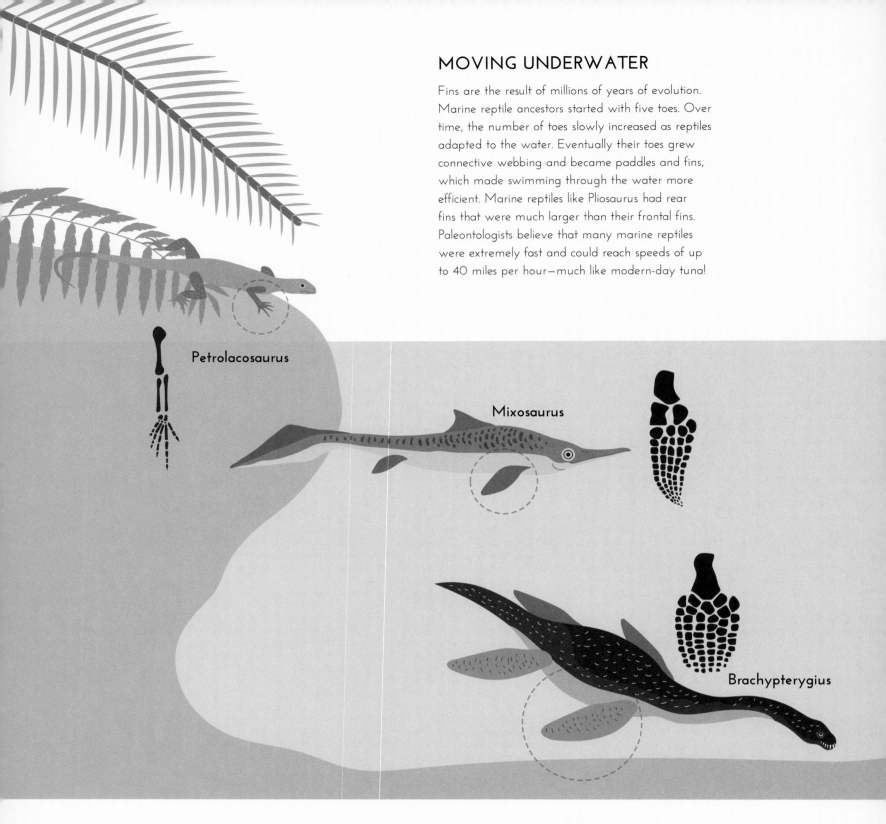

Petrolacosaurus

Mixosaurus

Brachypterygius

LONG AND SHORT NECKS

Pliosaurus and Plesiosaurus were very closely related. The former had a large head and a heavy body, while the latter was slimmer and more graceful. The length of their necks is what distinguished them. Plesiosaurus had a small head supported by a very long neck (made up of many vertebrae). Pliosaurus had a shorter neck that made it look almost like an alligator.

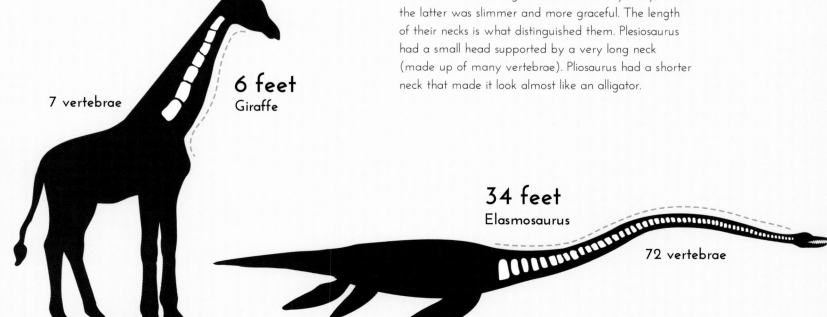

7 vertebrae

6 feet
Giraffe

34 feet
Elasmosaurus

72 vertebrae

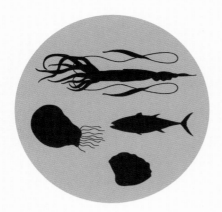

DIET

Marine reptiles were generally equipped with lots of large teeth, as they were mainly predators. Depending on their size and the depth in which they lived, they would eat other reptiles, fish, ammonites (a type of extinct mollusk), and belemnites (a type of extinct squid).

BIG EYES

In the animal kingdom, the size of the eye is usually related to the size of the body. However, many species of ichthyosaurs had enormous eyes given their body sizes. For example, Ophthalmosaurus was 13 feet long, but its eye had a diameter of 9 inches. That's the size of a dinner plate! The biggest eye belonged to the Temnodontosaurus. The reptile was 29 feet long, and its eye was 10 inches wide. It shares the record for the largest eye with the modern-day giant squid.

Such enormous eyes allowed these animals to explore depths of the ocean where the sunlight didn't reach. In many marine reptiles, the eye was surrounded by a bony ring, which was most likely meant to protect against the strong pressure experienced when swimming in such deep waters.

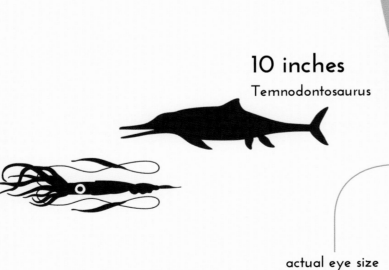

10 inches
Temnodontosaurus

actual eye size

0.9 inch
Human

GLOSSARY

PP. 6/7 **PALEOZOIC** — Geological era that was 540 to 248 million years ago. It means "ancient life."

MESOZOIC — Also called the "Age of Reptiles," it was 251 to 65 million years ago. It means "middle life" and its end marked the extinction of dinosaurs.

CENOZOIC — It was 65 to 2 million years ago. Also known as the "Tertiary Age" or the "Age of Mammals," it means "new life."

DIAPSIDS — All reptiles (except for turtles). Their skulls had two holes in the back and two holes behind the eyes.

SYNAPSIDS — All mammals and some prehistoric reptiles, like Pelycosaurs. They had only one hole on each side of their skulls.

ANAPSIDS — All turtles. They have no holes on the sides of their skulls.

PP. 8/9 **PALEONTOLOGIST** — Scientists who study the fossilized remains of creatures from the past.

SAURISCHIA — "Reptile-hipped" dinosaurs that include theropods and sauropods.

ORNITHISCHIA — "Bird-hipped" dinosaurs. They were plant-eaters, often with feet similar to hoofs.

THYREOPHORA — Ornithischia dinosaurs equipped with defensive spikes and bony plates. They included Stegosaurus and Ankylosaurus.

THEROPODS — Two-legged carnivorous dinosaurs with claws. "Theropod" means "feet of the wild beast."

SAUROPODS — Enormous four-legged dinosaurs with long necks, small heads, and long tails. They were plant-eaters.

DINOSAURS — Terrestrial reptiles that lived in the Mesozoic era and walked upright. Birds evolved from them. The word "dinosaur," which means "terrifying lizard," was coined by Sir Richard Owen in 1841.

ARCHOSAURS — The reptiles that ruled the Earth during the Mesozoic era. They include crocodiles, pterosaurs, dinosaurs, and birds.

GROUPS, SUBORDERS, FAMILIES, SUBFAMILIES, GENUS, SPECIES — From largest to smallest, these are the levels of classification for living creatures. The smaller the level, the more alike the creatures are.

PP. 10/11 **TRIASSIC** — The first period of the Mesozoic era (251-204 mya), when the first dinosaurs and the first mammals began to appear.

JURASSIC — The middle period of the Mesozoic era (204-146 mya). Dinosaurs dominated the Earth, and the first plants with flowers began to appear.

CRETACEOUS — The last period of the Mesozoic era (146-65 mya). It ended with a mass extinction that included dinosaurs and many other animals and plants.

PANGAEA — The supercontinent that assembled all the landmass on Earth. It existed from the end of the Paleozoic era to the Jurassic period.

PANTHALASSA — The huge ocean that surrounded Pangaea. It lasted until Pangaea broke apart.

PP. 12/13 **LAURASIA** — The big northern continent that formed during the Jurassic period, when Pangaea broke apart. It included the lands that now are now North America, Europe, Asia, Greenland, and Iceland.

GONDWANA — The big southern continent that resulted from the division of Pangaea. It was formed by the lands that are now Africa, India, Australia, and Antarctica.

K-T EXTINCTION — The mass extinction that occurred 65 mya, between the end of the Cretaceous (K) period and the beginning of the Tertiary (T) period.

P. 16 **FOSSILS** — The remains of ancient organisms preserved inside rocks.

P. 18 **CELLULOSE** — The polysaccharide that forms the main structure of plants. Digesting it usually takes a long time.

GASTROLITHS — Stones that certain animals ingest to help grind hard plant matter inside their stomachs.

P. 27 **ORNITHOMIMIDAE** — Dinosaurs similar to ostriches, with long legs. They lived about 76-65 mya. They had toothless beaks and fed on meat. Their name means "bird-mimics."

BONY PLATES — P. 28
Bony structures that grew on the bodies of some dinosaurs as a form of protection.

PACK — P. 46
A group of animals that gathers and cooperates to have more success in actions like hunting or taking care of their young.

COOPERATION
Mutual work toward a common goal.

NODULES — PP. 32/22
Small, rounded protuberances on the skin of some reptiles.

PLUME
Much softer than feathers. They cover the body and help keep it warm.

DOWN
The plumes that cover hatchlings when they can't fly yet.

FILOPLUME
A long, thin, and very flexible feather. It can play a role in the sensorial perception of stimuli (sensorial function).

FOSSIL SITE
A place in which the fossilized remains of ancient organisms have been discovered.

SEXUAL DIMORPHISM — P. 48
Differences in certain characteristics (size, color, shape, etc.) between the males and females of the same species.

FLAPPING FLIGHT — P. 48
Requires using the chest muscles to move the wings.

PASSIVE FLIGHT
A form of flight that doesn't require energy (the wings only aid in gliding).

ARBOREAL THEORY — P. 53
Explains the origin of flight as animals leaping from tree branch to tree branch.

TERRESTRIAL THEORY
Explains the origin of flight as animals running on land with occasional leaps that grew in distance.

PIGMENTS — P. 34
Natural substances present in living organisms that determine color.

PATAGIUM — P. 53
A membrane of skin stretched between the body and the limbs that allows animals to glide.

CLAW — P. 37
A sharp, pointy nail typical of predators.

CLASSIFICATION — P. 58
The system used by scientists to order all living beings. All animals are organized into categories or groups on the basis of common characteristics.

SEDIMENT — P. 39
Layers of rocks and minerals that may contain fossils.

NESTING AREAS — P. 40
Places chosen by animals to build nests in.

AMMONITES — PP. 62/63
Ancient mollusks with tentacles and coiled shells. Similar to the modern nautilus. The name comes from the Egyptian god Ammon, who was depicted with ram's horns that resemble the shells of these animals.

BELEMNITES
Ancient mollusks similar to squids, with internal shells shaped like bullets. They were predators and at the same time preyed on by many marine reptiles.

CATACLYSM — P. 45
A natural (and sudden) catastrophe, such as an earthquake, a volcanic eruption, a flood, or the impact of a meteorite.

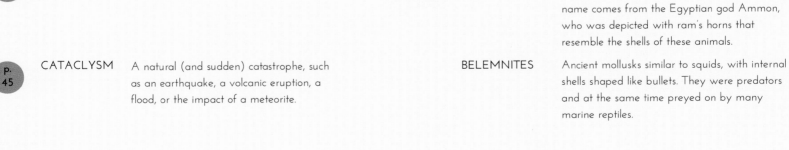

Argentinosaurus

T. rex

Apatosaurus

Maiasaura

Supersaurus

Iguanodon

Pachycephalosaurus

Parasaurolophus

Lambeosaurus

Psittacosaurus

DINOSAURS

Spinosaurus

Baryonyx

Centrosaurus

Tarbosaurus

Brachiosaurus

Cryolophosaurus

Edmontosaurus

Monolophosaurus jiangi

Styracosaurus

Ankylosaurus

Velociraptor

Utahraptor

Dromaeosaurus

Bajadasaurus

Stegosaurus

Diplodocus

Microraptor

Gallimimus

Anchiornis

Sinosauropteryx

Oviraptor

Ornithomimus

Pentaceratops

Triceratops

Kentrosaurus

Terzinosaurus

Yi qi

Serokonis

Parvicursor

Epidextipteryx

PTEROSAURS

Pteranodon

Nemicolopterus crypticus

Anhanguera

Quetzalcoatlus

Dimorphodon

MARINE REPTILES

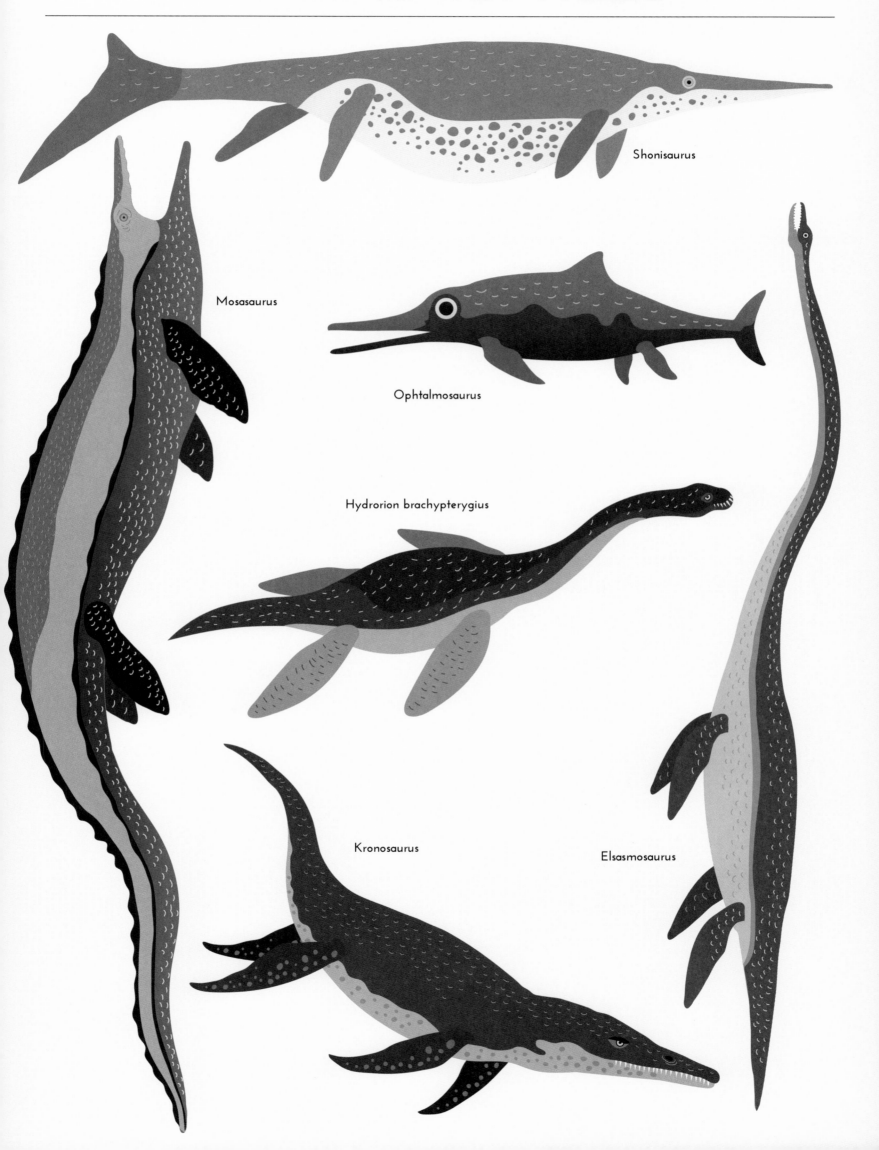

Shonisaurus

Mosasaurus

Ophtalmosaurus

Hydrorion brachypterygius

Kronosaurus

Elsasmosaurus

Giulia De Amicis

After completing a master's degree in Communication Design in 2012, Giulia began working as a visual designer and illustrator. Her work primarily consists of presenting information visually for newspapers, magazines, and associations in the environmental sector, with a particular focus on marine ecology, geography, and human rights. She has recently illustrated several titles for White Star Kids.

Cristina Banfi

Cristina Banfi graduated from the University of Milan with a degree in Natural Sciences. She has taught in several schools and worked for almost 20 years in the field of scientific communication, with an emphasis on ludo-didactic. She has also edited many scientific publications, particularly for young adults and children. During the last few years, she has published several titles with White Star.

Graphic layout by
Silvia Galliani

This edition first published by Shelter Harbor Press by arrangement with White Star s.r.l.

Cataloging-in-Publication Data has been applied for and may be obtained from the Library of Congress.

ISBN: 978-1-62795-164-7

Originally published by White Star Kids® which is a registered trademark property of White Star s.r.l.

© 2020 White Star s.r.l.
Piazzale Luigi Cadorna, 6 20123 Milan, Italy
www.whitestar.it

Translation: Inga Sempel
Editing: Leo Costigan

SHELTER HARBOR PRESS

603 W. 115TH STREET, SUITE 163
NEW YORK, NY 10025
www.shelterharborpress.com

For sales in the US and Canada, please contact info@shelterharborpress.com

Printed and bound in Heshan, China

10 9 8 7 6 5 4 3 2 1